Joy in Believing

Joy in Believing

SELECTIONS FROM THE
Spoken and Written Words
and the Prayers of
HENRY SLOANE COFFIN

EDITED BY WALTER RUSSELL BOWIE

CHARLES SCRIBNER'S SONS NEW YORK

2 42
C

PRINTED IN THE UNITED STATES OF AMERICA A-7.56[H]

Library of Congress Catalog Card Number 56-10345

228

ᴥᴥ Contents

Contents

✑ Preface

"Joy in believing": these words that St. Paul wrote in his letter to the Christians in Rome are the title of this book because they so exactly represent the spirit of that vivid contemporary Christian whose faith this book reflects. Henry Sloane Coffin, as anyone who ever saw him knows, rejoiced in the Lord. Tall and handsome, eager and brilliant in thought and speech, drawing people to him not only by the fascination of his mind but by the warmth of his outgoing interest, he was marked by nature for a happy life. But the happiness that might come from temperament and favoring circumstance is a lesser thing than joy. Happiness is like the glint of sunlight on the surface of a river; joy is like the living current of that river, which pours in its deep channel to the sea. That was the kind of vibrant joy that men felt in Henry Coffin. It was not only that he had the gift of human gaiety; he had the power that came from his trust in the unfailing springs of the grace of God. Only in the strength of that could he have accomplished his manifold ministry in a generation when the faith of many wavered before the hard facts of the Twentieth Century world. Henry Coffin never evaded those facts; but in his own experience he knew a mightier Fact. So in his long, rich pastorates in New York City; as

President of Union Seminary; as preacher in colleges and universities; as Moderator of the General Assembly of the Presbyterian Church U. S. A.; as champion of social right-eousness in many causes and on many platforms; as spokes-man and ambassador of Christian faith at critical moments both of peace and war not only in the United States but in Great Britain and in the Orient—he brought to numberless people new assurance of God and of the meaning of life through Him.

Books by Dr. Coffin that were published in his life time are well known, supremely, perhaps, "The Meaning of the Cross." When he died, what he had written in the course of many years was in his files. It was the privilege of the writer of this preface to find there and to read the long succession of Dr. Coffin's sermons and addresses, of which only a very few had appeared in any of his books; and the rich treasury of his prayers, none of which had been pub-lished before. From all these were gathered excerpts which might convey at least some of the great aspects of Henry Coffin's faith. If the words thus chosen to be put into print can transmit the spirit of the great Christian who wrote them, then to the readers of this book, as to those who once listened to his voice, there may come "joy in believing."

WALTER RUSSELL BOWIE

In the Beginning, God

On the first day of January, 1797, Horatio Nelson, then a captain on a ship in the Mediterranean, wrote his father: "My dear Father, on this day I am certain you will send me a letter." It is a touching indication of the often-forgotten family affection which lies behind and helps to account for a brilliant career. Nelson, no boy but a man of thirty-nine, knew that his father would not forget him, and on New Year's Day would send him a message. Sons and daughters of a far more devoted and faithful Father can surely look up, as we stand at the outset of another stretch of life's untried way, and tell Him: "On this day I am certain Thou hast a word for me."

It is a great thing to begin the year listening. Most of our regrets can be attributed to heedlessness. We meant well, but certain things did not occur to us; and very little can occur to the inconsiderate. God will not intrude Himself upon us; He stands at the door and knocks. Rarely He may seem to step into our lives uninvited; but that is when He meets us on some path, and blocks the way, or lays an arresting hand upon our shoulder. Otherwise He invariably knocks, and the rap of the Divine hand is so light that only an attentive ear within is aware that God is there. He comes on the wings of memories, in recollections of hallowed experiences or of saintly lives, in poignant regrets, in impulses and intuitions that well up we know not whence. He comes on the lips of a friend, in an event that astonishes us, in an unexpected happiness or sorrow, in the result of some long forgotten folly which comes home to us, in a solemn moment, like the passing of an old year, which faces us with ultimate questions such as "What are you amounting to?"; and at such times we are made to think. Then to our thoughtfulness, if it be Christian thoughtfulness, a thoughtfulness ruled by the Spirit of Jesus, comes the authentic personal word of the living God. "My dear Father, on this day I am certain you will send me a letter."

◢§ THE FIRE OF GOD

Is there really a more comforting text in the entire Bible than this: "Our God is a consuming fire"? What a guarantee it gives us for a clean earth! There is so much hampering rubbish in the world—false notions, unjustified prejudices, outworn conventions, obsolete barriers sundering those who should see eye to eye and work side by side—splendid material for a bonfire, and it is just waiting for the touch of the presence of the living God. Let Him in, and it will go up in a blaze.

What a hope it gives us for ourselves! Is there any more awful sentence than that in the concluding vision of the seer on Patmos: "He that is unjust, let him be unjust still: and he which is filthy, let him be filthy still"? We think of water as the symbol of cleansing, but those of us who go camping in our vacations know that a camp site is never left clean until all the odds and ends that litter the place are collected and put on the fire. When we look at ourselves are we not littered with unsightly things? Here are grudges left over from embittering experiences, the shells and husks of old beliefs from which the food has gone, remnants of our unconsecrated selves—the parts of ourselves which we have not known how to use or which we have not been willing to let others use. We need a blazing fire to make an end of this unlovely refuse. And that is exactly what God will be to us. If He let us alone and suffered us to remain as we are, He would not be love to us. The very height of His love is that He is a consuming fire. Let Him really come close to us in the cross of Jesus Christ and see what happens, see if much about our lives at this moment is not burned up as sheer debris, see if our hearts do not mount many degrees in temperature, reaching the boiling point of intolerance for things that ought not to be let continue, and caring intensely for everything that furthers the reign of Christ.

The demand of the hour is for a change in temperature among those who claim to be aligned with God. Science has made interesting discoveries of the effect of greater warmth on some organisms. There is a Chinese primrose which reared at under seventy degrees Fahrenheit has red flowers. Reared in a greenhouse at from eighty to ninety degrees Fahrenheit, its flowers become snow white. No heart is pure until it is passionate. Had we churches made up of people who were far hotter for the cause of Christ, we should show the world far finer Christians. The white flower of a blameless life is only produced when that life is warmed to ardent devotion.

⋙ FORGIVENESS AND RESTORATION

Fellow-sinners, with bitten and tattered years behind us—years blasted by conceit, or wasted in drifting or consumed in self-serving—the Gospel does not make it easy for us by saying: "Never mind the past; it can be wiped out; so forget it." God may cast our sins behind His back, and remember them no more against us. Christ may say to us tenderly: "Neither do I condemn thee: go in peace." But the record stands—the pathetic record of what we might have been and might have done in days that are no more. Rossetti put the tragedy of locust-eaten years in the sonnet:

> *The lost days of my life until today,*
> *What were they, could I see them on the street*
> *Lie as they fell? Would they be ears of wheat*
> *Sown once for food, but trodden into clay?*

5

Or golden coins squandered and still to pay?
Or drops of blood dabbling the guilty feet?
Or such spilt water as in dreams must cheat
The undying throats of hell, athirst alway?

I do not see them here; but after death
God knows the faces I shall see,
Each one a murdered self, with low last breath.
"I am thyself,—what hast thou done to me?"
"And I—and I—thyself," (lo, each one saith,)
"And thou thyself to all eternity!"

"And thou thyself"—that is appalling when one sees the very soil of one's nature the breeding-place of these pests of pride and shiftiness and all-absorbing egotism. "Thou thyself." "Lord, remember *me*." It is the past, an inalienable part of ourselves, which we ask Jesus to remember. Can't you hear his terrifying yesterdays pushing that penitent thief closer to Christ in his desperate need—the starved years calling "Remember me"?

And this is the Gospel: "Thou, thyself to all eternity, shalt be with Me." All that is ourself—the locust-eaten years, the soil where the larvae are hatched and from which they crawl to devour—all that is now with Christ and under His control, so that He can handle and restore it. He takes our pride and makes it reverence; our easy-going good nature and transmutes it into persuasive love; our self-regard and changes it to self-dedication. His forgiveness is companionship, companionship with us and with all that the past has accumulated in us. And such companionship redeems, because by being with us He gives us Himself: "I live, yet no longer I, but Christ liveth in me."

✑ THE CONSEQUENCES OF BELIEF

Thomas Fuller, a sixteenth-century divine dealing with prayer, has a sentence on Ejaculations which he defines as "short prayers darted up to God on emergent occasions," and he writes: "In barred havens, so choked up with the envious sands, that great ships, drawing many feet of water, cannot come near, lighter and lesser pinnaces may freely and safely arrive. When we are time-bound, place-bound, or person-bound, so that we cannot compose ourselves to make a large, solemn prayer, this is the right instant for ejaculations, whether orally uttered, or only poured forth inwardly in the heart." Call them what you will, thoughts that leap on the instant to God, find Him. What we want for the New Year is not merely an overruling Providence, who can repair our mistakes, nor only a wise Preparer of good works for us to walk in: we have both in a preceding and following Father. But better yet is His comradeship. "The Lord thy God is with thee, whithersoever thou goest—a very present help in trouble."

"Therefore." One of the great features of the Bible's men of faith is their logic. They state their premises, and then they go on to draw the inevitable conclusions. So many of us have our convictions, but never make the necessary inferences. We have got to learn to use the "therefore." "I believe that I have a Father, therefore I shall not love as a worrying, lonely, uncared-for orphan." "I possess a Refuge, therefore nothing shall rob me of serenity." "I am in a stronghold, therefore no pressure shall force me to fall back." "There are infinite reinforcements ready to come on the field at a moment's notice, therefore I shall never have the faintest hesitation in holding out on the front line of Christian principles." "Therefore" is a formal sort of word we do not often use in ordinary conversation. It sounds a bit stiff.

Well, so much the better for our religious thinking, for stiffening is just what we most need.

✍§ RELIGION THAT LIFTS

Isaiah 46:1, 3 & 4—"Bel boweth down, Nebo stoopeth; their idols are upon the beasts, and upon the cattle, the things that ye carried about are made a load, a burden to the weary beast. Hearken unto me, O house of Jacob, and all the remnant of the house of Israel, that have been borne by Me from their birth, that have been carried from the womb; and even to old age I am He, and even to hoar hairs will I carry you; I have made and I will bear; yea I will carry and will deliver."

Here is a contrast between gods that men carry and a God who carries men, between religion as a load and religion as a lift. The prophet draws a graphic picture of the clumsy images of the gods of Babylon bobbing and swaying in an absurdly undignified fashion on the backs of straining and sweating beasts, as their frightened devotees try to take them off to a place of safety before the invading Persians. "Things you lug about," he derisively labels the deities of these image-revering Babylonians. And he contrasts them with the living God of Israel's experience, who had taken the nation in His arms at its birth in Egypt and had been carrying it ever since. "Even to old age I am He, and even to hoar hairs will I carry you; I have made, and I will bear; yea, I will carry and will deliver."

To us likewise the prophet would say that a burdensome religion is a false religion; that a god whom we conceive in doctrines which we force ourselves to believe and which we struggle to safeguard, with whom we have fellowship in forms we must spur themselves to keep up, and whom we serve in duties our consciences strap on their reluctant backs, is a man-made idol, not the living and true Lord of heaven and earth. Religion that is a load is not comradeship with the Most High God. Religion which you must take care of is not the faith you need, but religion which takes care of you. The test by which one may discover whether he is dealing with an idol or with the living God is this: Do you feel yourself carrying your religion, or is it carrying you? Is it a weight or wings?

A Christian's beliefs are not ideas which he compels his intellect to accept; they are convictions—ideas which grip and hold him. They seem to come with hands and arms and to grasp his reason; he is aware of being lifted and carried along by them. The Truth takes him off his feet, and he is conscious of resting on it, rather than on ground of his own choosing. He may struggle and attempt to free himself, but sooner or later he admits: "I can't get away from the belief that . . . I am compelled to feel that it is reasonable to think that." And after he has been carried some years, it never occurs to him to break loose from these convictions; he is sustained by them, and upborne with serene satisfaction.

PRAYERS

O God, who wast and art and art to come, we bless Thee for our hope of Thine advent to accomplish Thy purpose and establish Thy reign of justice and peace. We know that in times past thou hast come, in truth which brought liberty, in righteousness which aroused consciences, in the downfall of tyrannies and in the fellowship of peoples, in the messages of seers and the lives of the faithful, above all in Thy Word made flesh in Thy Son. Awaken us to watch for Thine arrivals; keep us ready to serve lest we be found unprofitable servants; enable us to make the crooked straight and the rough places plain for an highway for Thee into the life of our time; and let our generation become a day of the Lord.

Most High God, who sent us the dayspring from on high to visit our earth, to gladden men's hearts and usher in a day of goodwill and peace, we rejoice in His light; and we wait for His yet fuller advent, when none shall sit in darkness and in the shadow of death and all feet shall walk in paths of peace, when Thy glory in His face shall be reflected from the work and ways of the whole world and all flesh see it together, when Thou who wast in Him Immanuel shalt be all in all. Number us, we beseech Thee, among those watchful servants who by plan and toil prepare the way of their Lord, and let us behold His Kingdom who is the desire of nations, the Prince of Peace, the Light of Life.

O God, whose comings always have taken men by surprise and who hast bidden us be ready, for in such an hour as we think not Thou appearest, keep us from complacency with things as they are lest our patience delay Thee; and prevent us from blindness to the gains of the past lest we fling away in haste that which long toil has acquired. Give us open minds and sound judgments, broadening sympathies which include ever more circles, and loyal hearts which hold steadfastly the trusts we have already assumed. Come to the sick with healing, to the lonely with companionship, to the happy with visions that consecrate their joys, to the strong with responsibilities, to the weak with obligations which develop strength, to the unfriended as the outreaching love revealed to us forever in Jesus Christ our Lord.

Through Perplexity to Faith

A typical soul of our time is unveiled for us in the letters of that brilliant young writer, Katherine Mansfield. Again and again she insists that she can't believe in a personal God. That is ruled out in the view of the world with which science faces us. But this leaves her an orphan spirit. "No, there's no God," she writes her husband. "That is queer. This morning I wanted to say 'God keep you' or 'Heaven guard us.'" Later, on a glorious day, she writes: "If only one could make some small grasshoppery sound of praise to *someone*—thanks to *someone*. But who?" Still again: "I believe the greatest failing of all is *to be frightened*. When I look back on my life all my mistakes have been made because I was afraid. Was that why I had to look on death? Would nothing less cure me? . . . You know one can't help wondering sometimes. . . . No, not a personal God, or any such nonsense. Much more likely —the soul's desperate chance." But she cannot settle to that. A year later she is telling another correspondent:

> It seems to me there is a great change come over the world since people like us believed in God. God is now gone for all of us. Yet we must believe; and not only that—we must carry our weakness and our sin and our devilishness to somebody. I don't mean in a bad abasing way. But we must feel that we are *known,* that our hearts are known, as God knew us. Therefore love today between lovers has to be not only human but divine. Their love is their religion. . . . But oh, it is no good.

And she speaks of her life in another letter as "thirty-two years in the dark."[1]

[1] Two volumes of Katherine Mansfield's letters have been published by Alfred A. Knopf, Inc., New York.

The Son of man is to come to seek and to save that which was lost. Jesus did not argue about God. He did not try to prove Him. He assumed that for which Katherine Mansfield, battling with tuberculosis and eager to write her books, was so wistful—that Love is the ultimate Force in and Meaning of the universe, the very nature of God. And Love is inconceivable apart from that which we call "personality." Jesus did not limit God by what He knew in man: to Him God is at least all that man is and more. God is all that we label "personality" *plus*. All that we know as love, plus. And Love craves companions. Love lives by and on sympathy, understanding, friendship. The explanation of this whole bewildering cosmos, evolving from stardust up to man, is the quest of God for some who will share His mind and be partners of His purpose.

Man's chief end, then, is to respond to Love, to trust Love wholly, and to discover Love's gifts to the responsive. Jesus never debated His discoveries. He gave His witness: "Verily I say unto you." You may have happened on a suggestive sentence in one of Keats' letters:

> Man should not dispute or assert, but whisper results to his neighbors.

He who did not strive nor cry aloud kept attesting with quiet assurance His results: "I say unto you." "Your heavenly Father knoweth." "God careth." "Blessed are the merciful: they obtain mercy." "Blessed are the pure in heart, they see God." "Knock, and it is opened unto you."

These were His "results," so patently "results" that countless thousands in the centuries since have seen the God He companied with embodied in Him, have found God and been found by Him seeking and saving them in Jesus.

✺§ BEYOND CYNICISM

This is patently not man's universe. He did not make it; he cannot fundamentally alter it. It does not ask either his approval or his censure. Liking or disliking, we have to take it. What, then, is it towards us? Is it "the nonchalant universe," Thomas Hardy called it? If so, thanksgiving is nonsense. How can we say: "O uncaring Cosmos, we thank Thee"?

There are not a few who think Hardy right, and are glad of it. Dependence on Another, in their judgment, keeps man infantile and slackens his effort to bring into being the society of his heart's desire. "Teach man," they say, "that in the teeth of an indifferent universe he must resolutely think out and build the commonwealth in which all nations and races shall find justice and the maximum satisfaction." That sounds heroic; but the self-made man, who is aware that he has carved his own career, is apt to be offensive. He "glories" as though he had not "received." And a man-made world —one has misgivings as to its quality and serious doubt as to the likeableness of its conscious creators.

Further, the fact must be faced that when the self-reliant suffer the strain and disheartenment of hope deferred, they frequently turn cynics. For on their premises what are men but ephemeral creatures whose careers are trivial incidents in the story of this many-million-yeared planet? Man, as they cannot help knowing him in themselves and in the specimens about them, is usually selfish, often stupid, always limited, and inclined to take himself with absurd seriousness. Hardy, the believer in a "nonchalant universe" addressed these stanzas to the Moon:

> "Have you much wondered, Moon,
> On your rounds,
> Self-wrapt beyond Earth's bounds"

"Yea, I have wondered, often wondered
*   At the sounds*
Reaching me of the human tune
*   On my rounds."*

"What do you think of it, Moon,
*   As you go?*
Is life much or no?"
"Oh, I think of it, often think of it
*   As a show*
God ought surely to shut up soon,
*   As I go."*

The dependent men, who live derivatively, taking their guidance, strength and courage from Another, and who live thankfully, face a different universe. Its Life and Lord is their Father, mysterious in His vastness, but who thinks on and cares for them. They feel themselves obliged to Him, and, however dubious and unapparent the advance here, they cannot relax their efforts or cease to toil and battle for the world they believe to be His heart's desire. To them life is never trivial; it is a solemn trust from God, and a trust with eternal significance, because begun here it continues with God forever and ever. They are under no illusions as to the perils and pathos of the passing show. "The whole world lieth in wickedness." But it is not meant to remain so. The loving God wills its redemption, and associates with Himself men and women who become sharers of His mind and partners of His patient labor.

GROWING OUT OF CHILDISHNESS

Man's self-confidence has been given a terrific jolt in these last years. This has been God's meeting us, if we have eyes to see Him. We shall not be less eager to work righteousness. But we shall envisage our part in our Father's business more modestly. Walking humbly with God has not been characteristic of modern Christians. When so many of our hopes have crashed, and so many of our designs have worked badly, or not worked at all; when we realize how impotent we are to control the civilization we prided ourselves on creating, and when that civilization itself is so unsatisfactory that there is no room left for pride; perhaps we shall talk less of ourselves as creators, and begin again to know ourselves creatures. "It is He that hath made us, and not we ourselves." "We are the clay, and Thou our Potter." Abraham Lincoln, with devout folk of an earlier day, habitually spoke of God as "My Maker." Instead of creators, we are at best tinkerers, sometimes helpful, sometimes blundering. Or in New Testament language, we shall recall that we are children, not adults. One might diagnose the disease of humanity as premature adolescence. We suddenly got it into our heads that within this mortal life man could cease to be a child, and could get on by himself and control his own destiny. What rubbish has been written about being masters of our fate and captains of our souls and creators of an ideal commonwealth! Such talk bowed God out of His universe, and put man on the throne. We have not realized that in threescore years and ten man does not pass much beyond the kindergarten stage, and that earth is populated by successive generations of children. Jesus assumed childishness even in the maturest pupils in His school, and said: "I will not leave you orphans." Independence and initiative are virtues in children, and should be fostered, but only up to a point; and they cannot be wisely fostered except within a home which rests on dependence and obedience.

❧ HOW CAN WE BELIEVE IN GOD?

Jesus defines our thought of God, but He does not confine it. God is like Jesus, but there is more in Him than could be revealed in any human life, as there is more in an ocean than a bay can contain. We supplement our thought of God in Christ from all man's experiences of the Highest. There are glimpses of the Father's face in all religions, for He has not left Himself anywhere without witness. There are outrayings of His light in every good life that earth has seen. There are revelations of Him in all things lovely. Shelley was expelled from Oxford University for a youthful avowal of atheism, but he professed himself a devotee of that "Beauty which penetrates and clasps and fills the world, scarce visible for extreme loveliness." And in that he was adoring the Christian God anonymously. There are contacts with Him through all the discoveries men make of His ways and works. Apart from Jesus, God would be vague: Jesus defines Him. But He will not allow us to limit God to what we see in Him: "The Father is greater than I."

This is the God whom the New Testament offers for our suffrages—like Jesus and greater.

But is there actually such a living God? There are three difficulties which are haunting the folk of our time concerning the reality of God. One is that He is a projection of man's wish. Certainly our thought of God is a projection. But so is our thought of any man. We understand another only by projecting our personality upon him, interpreting his feelings by our feelings, his thoughts by our thoughts. But because our thought of our neighbor is such a projection, that does not hinder him from being a living and real companion.

Another difficulty is that it may be said that God exists

only as a notion at the back of our own heads. God is an ideal of our evolving. He certainly is a notion in our minds; He could not be in our minds in any other way. You and I exist for each other as notions at the back of each other's heads. You say you see me; but what you see is a tiny image, which the light rays are refracting upon the retinae of your eyes, and which your nerves are transmitting to that mysterious interpreter we call the mind. Through these tiny images, so transmitted and interpreted, all life's intercourse goes on: we do business, we form friendships, we fall in love. What keeps coming to us through the image, and the consequent enrichments of life which ensue, are to us the evidences that the image is no delusion, but corresponds to a living person. Just so men have formed images of the mysterious Being whom they thought they found in the universe. There has been a struggle for existence and a survival of the fittest among the images of Deity—a struggle still on wherever the image of Christ as the symbol of the Highest is pitted with some other image. That image through which men derive the most, by means of which they find themselves most wisely and powerfully equipped to meet the demands of life, approves itself as corresponding to the Lord of life. If through the image of Christ one receives redemption from real sins, guidance in real perplexities, strength for real ordeals, a love which is as strong as death and stronger, he is not likely to question the correspondence of that image with a living and true God.

But although there come times when one is sure of God, there are also times of faltering and doubt. And our third difficulty is just there. Why should not God prove Himself to us beyond question? There is no proof of any of life's greatest goods. No one can demonstrate the beauty of a spring day: it is self-evident or it does not exist for us. No one can convince us of the desirableness of a friend or of the height, depth, length and breadth of a wife's love. These we know for ourselves. It is so of God. There is no proof that He is or that He loves. He comes to us along some one of His thousand paths and lays hold of us, and we respond. There is no proof; but there is social corroboration. Some of you may be familiar with the city of Portland, Oregon. Within sight, north, east, and south, are great mountain peaks which lift their summits ten thousand feet towards the blue. The whole city is laid out to command one or more of these views—its avenues, its squares, the sites of houses, their porches and baywindows are planned to provide prospects of these lofty hills of God. It so happens that though I have been twice in Portland, I never had sight of these peaks. Once summer heat shrouded the landscape in haze, and once forest fires blotted out all views with smoke. But I believe the mountains are there. It is not only that they are charted on the map, but that one cannot fancy several hundred thousand sensible Americans generation after generation drawing inspiration and buying and selling real estate on the basis of a delusion. Had I remained longer, I am sure I should have seen the mountains. And here are ten thousand times ten thousand, out of every century in our earth's history, grounding their lives on the assumption that they can lift their eyes higher than any hills to the Most High God, basing their institutions, their customs, their principles upon Him, claiming to draw from Him a wealth of spiritual life—courage, tenderness, a passion for justice, humility, reverence, self-sacrifice, indomitable hope. And this they do age after age.

✑ FINDING GOD

A test of the correctness of our inference based on experience is its practical value; the way in which it works in life. "He that willeth to do His will, shall know," Coleridge bursts out indignantly: " 'Evidences of Christianity!' I am weary of the word. Make a man feel the want of it; rouse him, if you can, to the self-knowledge of the need of it; and you may safely trust it to its own evidence." Religion approaches men saying, "O taste and see that the Lord is good." He cannot be good unless He *is*. A fancied Deity, an invention however beautiful of man's brain, cannot be a blessing, but, like every other falsehood, a curse. If our religion is a stained glass window we color to hide the void beyond, then in the name of things as they are, whether they have a God or not, let us smash the deceiving glass, and face either the darkness or the daylight outside. "Religion is nothing unless it is true." And its workableness is the test of its truth. Behind the accepted hypothesis of science lie countless experiments; and anyone who questions an hypothesis is simply bidden to repeat the experiment and convince himself. Behind the fundamental convictions of Christians lie generations of believers who have tried them and proved them. The God and Father of Jesus Christ is a tested hypothesis; and he who questions must experiment, and let God convince him. To commit one's self to God in Christ and be redeemed from most real sins, turned from selfishness to love, released from slavery to freedom; to trust Him in most real difficulties and perplexities, and find one's self empowered and enlightened, is to discover that faith works, and works gloriously. "Come and ye shall see." A man's idea of God may be most inadequate, but it is an idea that corresponds not to nothing existent, but to Someone

21

most alive. That which comes to us through the idea is witness of the Reality behind it.

Nor are we confined to the witness of our personal discoveries. There is a social attestation of the workableness of our faith. The surest way of establishing the value of our religious experience is to share it with another; the strongest confirmation of the objective existence of Him with whom we have to do is to lead another to see Him. The most effective defender of the faith is the missionary. "It requires," as David Livingstone said, "perpetual propagation to attest its genuineness." Not they who sit and study and discuss it, however cleverly, discover its truth; but they who spend and are spent in attempting to bring a whole world to know the redeeming love of One who is, and who rewards with indubitable comradeship with Himself those who prove wholeheartedly loyal.

✑§ HOW FAITH DEVELOPS

The capacity for religious experience can be cultivated. Faith, like an ear for music or taste in literature, is a developable instinct. It grows by contagious contact with fellow-believers; as "the sight of lovers feedeth those in love," the man of faith requires the stimulus of the believing Church. It is increased by familiarity with fuller and richer experiences of God; continuous study of the Bible leads men into its varied and profound communion with the Most High. It is enlarged by private and social worship; prayer and hymn and message were born in vital experiences, and they reproduce the experience. Browning, in characteristic verse, describes the effect of the service upon the worshippers in Zion Chapel Meeting:

> *These people have really felt, no doubt,*
> *A something, the motion they style the Call of*
> *them;*

And this is their method of bringing about,
By a mechanism of words and tones,
(So many texts in so many groans)
A sort of reviving and reproducing,
More or less perfectly, (who can tell?)
The mood itself, which strengthens by using.
And how that happens, I understand well.
A tune was born in my head last week,
Out of the thump-thump and shriek-shriek
Of the train, as I came by it, up from Man-
chester;
And when, next week, I take it back again,
My head will sing to the engine's clack again.

An unexpressed faith dies of suffocation, while utterance intensifies experience and leads to fresh expression; religion, like Shelley's skylark, "singing still doth soar, and soaring ever singeth." Above all, the instinct for the Unseen is developed by exercise; obedience to our heavenly visions sharpens the eyes of the heart. Charles Lamb pictures his sister and himself "with a taste for religion rather than a strong religious habit." Such persons exclude themselves from the power and peace, the limitless enrichment, of conscious friendship with the living God. They never come to know Him.

ᥱᏚ SPIRITUAL COMPANIONSHIP

In the course of human history there are epochs of doubt and epochs of faith. It is the spiritual atmosphere of the age which befogs or clarifies the living God. In 1867 John Addington Symonds in the course of a most frank letter to a friend wrote: "I have tried to show how the sentiment of God disappeared from me without the need of God being destroyed. But this is not a merely personal history, it is the history of the age in which we live, of the age of the disintegration of old beliefs. A man like myself can only lose his religious sentiment because the religious sentiment is weak in the men around him."

You and I cannot expect a satisfactory intercourse with the Invisible save as we keep company with men and women who are very sure of God. Thomas had no inkling of the presence of the living Christ in Jerusalem so long as he remained by himself and kept thinking over his difficulties. It was when he found himself with his convinced companions in the Upper Room that he discovered himself once more face to face with his Lord. If any man would like to have contact with the Most High, if fellowship with the Lord of heaven and earth seems to him desirable, and if with all his thinking about it, he cannot make the connection, let him share the experiences of those who have first-hand touch with God. If no living believers are available, we have always our predecessors of long ago, especially the men of the Bible, and their successors through the Christian centuries. Many a man who has lost hold of God has found himself gripped again through a page of the Gospel or a psalm or one of the letters of St. Paul. But living epistles are more effective, and we appreciate the pages of the written Bible best as they seem connected with similar experiences in men and women at our side. Go where praying people are; talk with those who sincerely feel themselves strengthened, enlightened, calmed, made glad, by their unseen Friend; share their life and work; and see whether the atmosphere about us does not become clearer. John Bunyan met some genuinely religious women at Bedford, and said: "I saw as if they were on the sunny side of some high mountain, there refreshing themselves with the pleasant beams of the sun, while I was shivering and shrinking in the cold." And it was not so long before he found himself in the same warming light.

THE SPRINGS OF GOD

One summer I happened to be with a group of men who were seeking a water supply for a cabin in the mountains. At the foot of the hill where the cabin was to be built there was what had long been thought a small spring from which ran a fairly steady trickle even on that August day. But the men in the group were of various minds about it. One allowed that he had always heard that there was a spring there, but now that he looked at it closely he thought it might be just the drainage of the hillside seeping down towards the brook whose almost parched bed lay below. Another, in corroboration of this doubt, called attention to the fact that there was not one trickle but several, and that they were some yards apart. A third thought that there was a spring there, and that it gave good water, but he questioned whether there was enough of it for the dependable supply of a household. But as no other source of water was as available, and as this spot had the reputation of containing a spring, for a piece of pipe had been placed there by somebody years ago for the convenience of trampers who wanted a drink, it was resolved to begin digging and explore. The diggers were astonished, after some shovelsful of topsoil had been removed and they got down to sand, to discover how abundant the flow, and how the various trickles when followed up converged into a single pool. And when the spring had been walled up with stone and concrete into a well-hole with a capacity of forty-eight gallons, it filled completely in three-quarters of an hour on a day in the last week of a dry August.

Men have always needed, and continue to need, a fountain of life—a supply of refreshment and invigoration and cleansing. For untold generations there has been a report, surprisingly widespread throughout the race, that there is a Spring of Living Water in the Invisible. Wayfarers have told of their finding it and drinking of it. But today mankind stands before this alleged Spring expressing diverse opinions concerning it. Some look contemptuously at the trickles, and declare them negligible for humanity's present needs. Some assert that such waters are injurious to social well-being—waters of Lethe lulling to sleep amid economic injustices. Others do not question that many in the past have slaked their thirst here, but consider this no adequate proof that it is a living Spring: it is the seepage of the spiritual idealism of the times which credulous souls have mistaken for a perennial flow. Others again point to the several trickles and doubt whether they come from a single source. But there continue to be a not inconsiderable company who regularly depend upon this Spring. While the rest are discussing it, they go on drawing from it. Surely their findings are the only evidence that matters.

And they—(may I not put it into the first person and say, and *we*?)—repeat the conviction of a frequenter of the Spring centuries ago: "To us there is one God, the Father, of whom are all things, and we unto Him." And we share His conviction that the various trickles converge to one pool where the fullness of the religious inspirations of the race becomes accessible to us, and then in some measure accessible through us. We hear a Voice: "If any man thirst, let him come unto Me and drink. He that believeth on Me, from within him shall flow rivers of living water." This is our "one Lord, Jesus Christ, through whom are all things, and we through Him."

ᴥ§ MAKING FAITH ARTICULATE

Apparently, we are passing out of a particular stage in the manifestation of personal religion. When we go back a couple of generations we find believing men and women quite frank in the expression of their fellowship with God. It did not seem forced to refer to Him in their letters, to gather their households together daily for family worship, to voice their religious experiences in prayer-meetings. This is not to say that there were more believers in proportion to the total population seventy-five or a hundred years ago, nor that a larger percentage were regular church-goers. Readers of the life of John Marshall must have been struck by the scanty church attendance in Washington in its early days as the national capital, and in 1795 the first Timothy Dwight is said to have found but one Church-member among the students at Yale. But those who were devout found it natural to express their intercourse with God. For a variety of reasons the religious life of the recent past has been tongue-tied. Men have shown their devotion in thousands of helpful ministries to human need. To be sure, there have been noteworthy men of prayer, but the majority of Christians have found no difficulty in accepting the Master's counsel to pray in secret. Family prayer has become an embarrassment to many a father and mother. God dropped out of general conversation. It has been bad form to mention one's personal relationship to Him. On the whole, this has been healthy, banishing cant and fostering reality. But there is a law of the human mind that expression deepens impression. An unmentioned God easily becomes an unthought-of God. A very large amount of our current religion is strictly anonymous. Men are devotees of right, loyal followers of consciences, good neighbors, public-spirited citizens, lovers of humanity—

only very rarely do they think of themselves as personally related to the Father in heaven. Now when we are not aware of a higher connection, the connection itself often becomes impaired. Engineers saw the relationship between the watershed in the Catskills and the needs of New York City, and built the new aqueduct. If another generation forgets where the water comes from, simply turns on the faucets or unscrews the hydrants, but pays no attention to maintaining the aqueduct in repair, there will be leaks and breaks, and the available supply of water will diminish. That has happened with our generation in its connections with the living God. We used the religious idealism we found at hand without concerning ourselves whence it came or how we could maintain a sufficient supply, and today we find ourselves with inadequate motive power to achieve our purposes. Whether we shall talk more of our fellowship with God is not the point; but it is evident that we must think more of it, and learn how to keep and employ it. How pitifully few of us have any idea of how to use our faith in God to surrender self-control, to maintain our serenity, to furnish us with patience, to reinforce our courage, to conquer our faults, to adjust us helpfully to His other children! A judgment is here. The profane persons, like Esau, without the faculty to establish the contact with the Invisible, judge themselves unworthy of the life which is open to men whose dreams lift them nearer to heaven and whose waking thoughts are set on possessing a covenant with the Most High. Those who see heaven opened, and who find the ladder reared at the exact spot where they are, those who have eyes and ears for the God and Father of Jesus Christ, are in command of incalculable resources unguessed by Esaus with their earthbound interests. We judge ourselves capable or incapable of companionship with our most companionable Father.

✑ THE INDISPENSABLE CHRIST

In a biography of Daniel Webster, there is an account of how he, an old man of seventy, visited his native New Hampshire, and met his brother-in-law, John Colby, whom he had not seen for forty-five years. Colby had been a reckless dare-devil and a problem in the family, "a loose-liver," in the vernacular of rural New England; but this mysterious Person who came into our world at Christmas had got hold of John Colby. The two old men met, and Colby, with Yankee directness, put a searching question to Webster. "You may be a *great* man; are you a *good* man?" And before they parted he asked the former Senator and Secretary of State to pray with him, and the two of them got down on their knees. Webster went home to say in amazement: "Why, miracles happen in these later days as well as in the days of old. John Colby has become a Christian."

There is a timid and apologetic spirit in the Church of today which holds us back from working such miracles of resurrection.

We are interested in and sympathetic with the various points of view of folk of our acquaintance who refuse to be called by the Christian name or to accord in their thought a place to Christ. We hesitate to commend our faith to them. It is certainly wholesome that we should distrust what is often labelled Christianity—a miscellaneous collection of beliefs and ethics and institution and usages, many of which have scant connection with the living faith and purpose of Jesus. But surely He Himself is the gift of God to every man the world over, as He is to you and me. We are not concerned that folk of other races and traditions should interpret Him precisely as we do: they cannot and will not. Many peoples have understood Him and spoken

29

of Him in their own way. We are not anxious to have them organize themselves in churches identical in form with ours: such churches might not serve their communities, and in any case this is a day for adaptable institutions. We do not care to have them worship in our manner: let them express their love and loyalty as they best can. Uniformity is deadening and impoverishing. But can there be any question of the necessity of their knowing Jesus, feeling the impress upon them of His person, entering on enriching friendship with Him? We need not disparage the spiritual life which any man or any nation already possesses apart from Him. They may be more alive than many nominal followers of Christ. But even so, can any man doubt the quickening effect of the touch of this Figure upon them? "He that hath the Son of God hath the life."

ᴥᔓ NEW LIFE IN DEATH VALLEY

The believers of the New Testament age and of every great age in the Christian Church witness to His power to make people over. Every one of us has defects and faults, disagreeable peculiarities, qualities which make us unlovely in our homes and difficult in business relations and annoying to our friends, and qualities which get in our own way and make us loathe ourselves. We do not wish to remain just as we are. God forbid! And this eagerness—(or is it hardly eagerness? Just a dull hope that some day we may be better)—this, whether strong or very weak, is the Spirit of God moving us. We must not resist Him by refusing. We must not impede Him by hanging on to our own follies and weaknesses. We must yield to Him and work with Him in disciplining ourselves. We can with His help be utterly different. Why not give Him His recreating way with us?

The Spirit of God can employ those willing to be employed whatever cost to them that may involve. It is just a matter of our self-abandonment. We cannot dictate the terms and say "I wish to be useful in this or that particular way." Or, "I am willing to be used to a certain extent." There must be a complete commitment of ourselves to His leading. And then no one can limit the results. Down deep within everyone of us is the wish to be used for the purposes of God in our generation. That wish is the sign of His Spirit. With such backing our wish can in His way come true.

In the newspapers a while ago there was an account of a marvellous happening out in our far western deserts. There is a gorge with the forbidding name of Death Valley, where in 1850 a party of immigrants, California-bound, perished from thirst. It is some 150 miles long and from ten to thirty-five miles wide, with bare sand dunes and buttes of tan and brown, and lying in such extreme heat that even the lizards and horned toads are said to leave it in summer. It is the lowest and hottest dry land in our western hemisphere. But for nineteen consecutive days not so long ago showers fell on that waste land—a thing unheard of before. All manner of seeds, apparently dormant for years, suddenly burst into bloom. Lilies, buttercups, poppies, larkspur, columbines, Indian paint brush, clothed it with yellows and reds and purples. A botanist reports one hundred varieties of flowers gathered in an half hour within a radius of fifty yards.

Who will say what is dormant in this Death Valley of our human world? What seeds there are in your heart and mine? The moisture of God's Spirit is always at hand, but atmospheric conditions usually keep it away or reduce it to insignificant proportions. The miracle waits until enough believing folk, or until a few folk who believe enough in the living God, change the spiritual climate. With the showers of His Spirit falling and falling consecutively, how fair our new world and how lovely its inhabitants! That is the Pentecost of love for which God longs. It is the Pentecost for which we long. Are we prepared to identify our wistfulness with the moving of His Spirit upon us, and by faith to open for Him the entrances He needs?

◄§ WHAT PRAYER MAKES POSSIBLE

When the apostle Peter was put in jail, "prayer was made earnestly of the church unto God for him." When he came to the house of John Mark's mother, he found folk praying. Many of us do not pray because we fancy ourselves confined within walls of inexorable law—economic, physical, psychological. The world on which we look out knows no other actors but these forces and men. A direct appeal to God seems absurd. Then an emergency forces us to pray. Usually it is the collision of our feelings with what seems to our intelligence the impossible. The Christians in Jerusalem found their affection for Peter obstructed by the stone walls of a prison. They prayed—prayed with no idea how their prayers would effect a result. What followed remained obscure to them, but confirmed their confidence in God. How He answered they had no explanation; they said that the iron gate "opened of its own accord."

Prayer to the most mature Christian is a mystery. The more sophisticated we become, the likelier we are not to pray except within narrow limits where we think we can find room for God to act. Most of us would consider it absurd to pray for the removal of an obstructing door. But is it certain that God has no means beyond those which we can itemize? Must we not always allow for His ability "to do exceeding abundantly above all that we ask or think"? In any case, is it not the attested fact of all Christian experience that when we pray a door opens, and we are face to face with One wiser than our wisest and better than our best?

Jesus taught: "Knock, and it shall be opened unto you." Prayer in His mind removed a barrier between man and God. There is an indefiniteness in the phrase "it shall be opened." Even to Jesus prayer was mysterious, but "dark with excess of bright." Prayer somehow lets God come in and act with His children; and whenever God is with us, the results and the means by which they are wrought are beyond our intelligence to account for.

৺ WHEN FAITH IS JUSTIFIED

To believe in a living and active God is to face life without worry or fear or pessimism. We think of movements in our generation which carry on the purpose of Jesus—transformations of the relations of races and nations, regenerations of economic groups in industry and commerce, ennoblements of the relationships of husband and wife in marriage and of parents and children in the home —transformations of these relationships until they begin to embody such reverent love as Jesus showed for man when He laid down His life for us. We think of the resolves in our own hearts to fill some role in these or similar causes. We cannot see enough wisdom or power at hand to achieve these ends. If we could, we should not need God. These Christlike purposes have their crucifixions and burials; and there is nothing for us but to depend on an invisible Ally. And such dependence is not misplaced. "To them that love, God worketh all things with them for good."

◢§ JOY IN THE LIVING GOD

It is a great thing to find believing people really using their faith. When Emily Brontë had died, and Anne lay stricken with the same fatal malady, Charlotte wrote to her friend, Miss Nussey: "I avoid looking forward or backward and try to keep looking upward. This is not the time to regret, dread or weep. What I have and ought to do is very distinctly laid out for me; what I want and pray for, is strength to perform it. The days pass in a slow, dark march; the nights are the test; the sudden wakings from restless sleep, the revived knowledge that one lies in her grave and another not at my side, but in a separate and sick bed. However, God is over all. Yours sincerely, C. Brontë." Thomas Carlyle often seemed to have little Christian faith, but that devout Scottish home at Ecclefechan where he was reared had stored his soul with treasures, and as life heaped its burdens on him he was driven to take them out and employ them. In his old age he wrote to Professor Charles Eliot Norton at Harvard: "Grief teaches one the measureless solitude o' life where everything is of no sort of avail, nor any comfort to be had except in a man's self; and not much there saving as the conviction is borne in on him that through mystery and darkness everything is ruled by One most Wise and most Good, and he learns to say in his heart, Thy will be done." O fellow-believers, take down from the shelf the religion we know and enjoy and put it into vigorous operation. Trust, trust, trust the living God! Plan trustfully, venture trustfully, work trustfully—give the living God the chance to be God to you and me.

PRAYERS *Sun morn.*

O God, in whom is no darkness at all, Thine is the glory of the morning, Thine the brightness upon our path from the wise and faithful and devout who have gone before us, and Thine the fulness of grace and truth which shine in the face of Jesus Christ. O Sun of righteousness, dispel the mists of doubt, burn away our selfishness, and guide us into Thy mind for us, that diligent in study, loyal in friendship, thankful for Thy gifts, devoted to our high calling, we may approve ourselves children of the day, through Thy mercy, whereby the dayspring from on high doth visit us and call us into His marvelous light.

O God, whose riches towards us in Christ Jesus are unsearchable, whose love is beyond our knowledge, whose peace passeth all understanding, and who art able to do exceeding abundantly above all that we ask or think, we praise Thee for the resources which are ours in Christ: for reserves of power upon which we can draw without limit, for a patience that fainteth not neither is weary, for a perseverance which seeks until it brings the wanderer home, for an understanding which knows us far better than we can know ourselves, for a reverence for us that trusts and honors us when we have lost self-respect and forfeited all confidence from others, for a forgiveness which stops at nothing, for a grace which is able to save unto the uttermost, for a love which beareth, believeth, hopeth, endureth all things and never faileth, for a fulness from which we receive grace upon grace and know that from its supplies we shall still receive until we are filled unto all the fulness of God. Oh, how great is Thy goodness, which Thou hast laid up for them that obey Thee in Christ

Jesus, which thou hast wrought and workest even until now in Christ for them that follow Him among the sons of men. Thanks be unto Thee for Thine unspeakable gift.

Sun. noon

O God, who crownest the year with Thy goodness, we praise Thee for the thought that planned our paths, the eye that watched our going, and the hand that never left us to walk alone. We thank Thee for all Thy blessings noticed and recalled, and more for unnoticed blessing; for the temptations into which we were not led; the prayers Thou didst love us too well to answer, for the mistakes we were kept from making, the sorrows we were spared, the limitations imposed on us to prevent us from wasting ourselves, the failures we might have made but for Thine unsuspected and unthanked for aid, for rough places where we might have stumbled made smooth and smooth places where we might have idled made rough; for hopes disappointed that we might hope for something nobler, plans upset that they might become less selfish, purposes thwarted that we might say, "Not as I will, but as thou wilt" and make a diviner purpose ours, for dear lives spared to us that we might serve them and be inspired by them, and for dear lives taken that we might rejoice in their larger life and have more home ties binding us to the world unseen and more interest in the things that last. Above all we thank Thee for another year of life with Christ and with Thee in Him—for an increasing share in His plans, a growing intimacy with His thought, a deepening sympathy with His love. Bless the Lord, O My soul, and forget not all His benefits.

Sun. eve.

Grant us, Almighty God, Thy peace that passeth understanding, that amid the storms and troubles of this our life we may rest in Thee, knowing that all things are in Thee, not beneath Thine eye only, but under Thy care, governed by Thy will, guarded by Thy love, so that with a quiet heart we may meet the storms of life, the cloud and the thick darkness, rejoicing to know that the darkness and the light are both alike to Thee. Guide, guard, govern us this day through Jesus Christ, our Lord.

*The Cross, and Its Light
on Human Suffering*

In a novel of Maurice Hewlett's a generation ago one of the servants of Coeur de Leon says to him:

"There was a Father, my lord King Richard, who slew His own Son, that the world might be the better."

"And was the world much the better?" asked the monarch.

"Beau sire," came the reply, "not very much. But that was not God's fault, for it had, and still has, the chance of being the better for it."

Yes, it has. And most of us know that the strongest force shaming us out of selfishness and drawing us into trust and love is the symbol of that death on a mound outside the walls of Jerusalem centuries ago.

People who live by a river rarely think of its source. Not many in the City of New York, dwellers on the banks of the Hudson, and indebted to that stream for the beauty and health of their neighborhood, can say exactly where the Hudson comes from. There is a tiny pool of a lake, lying some four thousand feet up in a mountain notch, about a thousand feet beneath the summit of Marcy, with the lovely name—Lake Tear of the Clouds—which is the ultimate source of this mighty and magnificent stream.

The origins of our fairest and most fruitful motives are as little known or thought of. Back of the qualities in men and women about us which make them admirable and serviceable, back of the cleansing forces which keep nations from stagnating in self-sufficiency and greed, back of the most generous thinking of our age and its best hopes for mankind, is that Life laid down at Calvary. "We love, because He first loved."

Rivers roll on and make beautiful and clean and fertile the countryside, whether men know or think of the source whence their waters come. And we cannot minimize the

41

inestimable consequences of the sacrifice of Christ which are quite unsuspected by the world for which He died. There is a stream of beauty in our art, our music, our literature, our common life, which would not be there, had not the Son of God given Himself on the cross. But such unsuspected connections are trifling in their results compared with a *recognized* debt. It is when we face the Crucified, and let His love unto the uttermost sink in on our heart and conscience, that rivers of living water—His own Spirit of devotion—well up and pour forth. Thanks not to anything in us, but thanks to Him we become different folk to live with, different inhabitants of this confused and grasping world, who in turn make it a different place for those who dwell in it today and will be here in many morrows.

✑§ REDEMPTION THROUGH SUFFERING

"Cor cordium" is the inscription placed upon Shelley's grave; and it is infinitely more appropriate for the Man of Nazareth. In His sensitive sympathy we are aware of

Desperate tides of the whole great world's anguish
Forc'd through the channels of a single heart.

We begin to understand more deeply the recoil of Jesus from the cross as we remember His sense of kinship with those who were reddening their hands with the blood of the representative of their God. If we have ever been beside a devoted wife in the hour when her husband is disgraced, or been in a home where sons and daughters are overwhelmed with a mother's shame, we have some faint idea of how Jesus felt the guilt of His people when they slew Him. He was the conscience of His less conscientious brethren: "The reproaches of them that reproached Thee fell on Me." He realised, as they did not, the enormity of what they were doing. The utter and hideous ungodlikeness of the world was expressed for Him in those who would have none of Him, and cried: "Away with Him! Crucify, crucify Him." His keenness of conscience and His acute sympathy brought to His lips the final cry: "My God, My God, why hast Thou forsaken Me?" The sinless Sufferer on the cross, in His oneness with His brethren, felt their wrong-doing His own, confessed in His forsakenness that God could have nothing to do with it for it was anti-God, owned that it inevitably separated from Him, and He felt Himself in such kinship and sympathy with sinning men that He was actually away from God. "That was hell," said old Rabbi Duncan, "and He tasted it."

But our minds revolt. We do not believe that God deserted His Son; on the contrary we are certain that He was never closer to Him. Shall we question the correctness of Jesus' personal experience, and call Him mistaken? We seem compelled either to do violence to His authority in the life of the spirit with God, or to our conviction of God's character. Perhaps there is another alternative. A century ago the physicist Young discovered the principle of the interference of light. Under certain conditions light added to light produces darkness; the light waves interfere with and neutralize each other. Is there not something analogous to this in the sphere of the spirit? Is not every new unveiling of God accompanied by unsettlements and seeming darkenings of the soul, temporary obscurations of the Divine Face?

And may it not have been God's coming closer than ever to the Son of His love, or rather the Son's coming closer to the Father, as He entirely shared and expressed God's own sympathy and conscience, and was made perfect by the things which He suffered, that wrought in His sinless soul the awful blackness of the feeling of abandonment?

In the sense of suffering sin's force, of conscientiously accepting its burden, of sensitively sympathising with the guilty, Jesus bore sin in His own body on the tree.

And as we stand facing the Crucified we cannot escape a sense of personal connection with that tragedy. The solidarity of the human family in all its generations has been brought home to us in countless ways by modern teachers; we are members one of another, and as we scan the cross this is a family catastrophe in which the actors are our kinsmen, and the blood of the Victim stains us as sharers of our brothers' crime.

And further as we look into the motives of Christ's murderers—devout Pharisee and conservative Sadducee, Roman politician and false friend, bawling rabble and undiscriminating soldiery, the host of indifferent or approving faces of the public behind them—they seem strangely familiar to us. They have been, they are still, alive by turns in us. The harmless spark of electricity that greets the touch of one's hand on a metal knob on a winter's day is one with the bolt of lightning that wrecks a giant oak. The selfish impulse, the narrow prejudice, the ignorant suspicion, the callous indifference, the self-satisfied respectability, which frequently dominate us and determine our decisions, are one with that cruel combination of motives which drove the nails in the hands and feet of the Son of God. Still further, the suffering of Jesus never seems to an acute conscience something that happened once, but is over now. The Figure that hung and bled on the tree centuries ago becomes indissolubly joined in our thought with every life today that is the victim of similar misunderstanding and neglect, injustice and brutality; and, while our sense of social responsibility charges us with complicity in all the wrong and woe of our brethren, that haunting Form on Calvary hangs before our eyes, and

44

Makes me feel it was my sin,
As though no other sin there were,
That was to Him who bears the world
A load that He could scarcely bear.

We may say to ourselves that this is fanciful, that we were not the Sanhedrin who condemned Jesus, nor the Roman procurator who ordered His execution, nor the scoffing soldier who carried out his command; but the conscience which the cross itself creates charges us with participation in the murder of the Son of God. That cross becomes an inescapable fact in our moral world, an element in our outlook upon duty, a factor touching life with tragic somberness. It forces upon us the conviction that it is all too possible for us to re-enact Golgotha, and by doing or failing to do, directly or indirectly, for one of the least of Christ's brethren, to crucify Him afresh and put Him to an open shame.

But if the cross seems to tinge life somberly, it also gilds it with glory. As we follow Christ we discover more and more clearly that all which we possess of greatest worth has come to us and keeps coming to us through Him. What He endured centuries ago on that hill outside the city wall is a wellspring of inspiration flowing up in the purest and finest motives in the life of today. There is a direct line of ancestry from the best principles in the lives of nations and of individuals about us running back to Calvary. Day after day we find ourselves and other men and the whole world made different because of that tragic occurrence of the past, shamed out of the motives that caused it, and lifted into the life of the Crucified. And with such an experience of inheriting our noblest life from that cross, we cannot say other than that, "He bore our sins in His own body on the tree, that we, being dead to sins, should live unto righteousness; by whose stripes ye were healed."

45

✎§ INTO THE MIDNIGHT BLACKNESS

To Jesus, as to ourselves, nature sometimes appeared morally neutral: its suns shone on evil and on good; its rains fell on just and on unjust. The tower of Siloam had tumbled on men no worse than their neighbors. And when one thinks of the horrors which today overtake the best no less than the worst, the innocent no less than the guilty, we question whether there be behind our indifferent universe a Power who is committed to righteousness and who cares for its servants. There are

> *Fallings from us, vanishings,*
> *Blank misgivings of the creature,*

what William James called "the sick shudder of the frustrated religious demand." We look up for sympathy, and nothing comes. Suppose God were letting His Son's life go for naught? Was not that the haggard doubt which dogged Jesus at the last, and wrung from Him the cry: "My God, why hast Thou forsaken Me?" He suffered being tempted to question the fidelity of God.

And this lonely cry speaks of a yet sorer pain. He was struggling with a moral confusion: "Why? Why?" Had He done rightly in coming to the capital and precipitating this struggle with the authorities? Was He justified in exposing the leaders of the nation to an act which would bring such appalling consequences for the whole people? He saw doom about to overwhelm His country: "Daughters of Jerusalem, weep not for Me, but weep for yourselves and for your children." "The days are coming in which they shall say to the mountains, Fall on us, and to the hills, Cover us." The vision of a desolated city, laid even with the ground and her children within her, haunted Him. And He had helped bring this on by coming up to Jerusalem.

The British historian, John R. Green, distressed by the policy the government of his day was following in foreign affairs, wrote in a letter:

> I love England dearly. But I love her too well to wish her triumphant if she fights against human right and human freedom. Pitt longed for her defeat in America, but it killed him when it came. I can understand that double feeling now.

Such a "double feeling" may render vivid to us our Lord's spiritual conflict. Hanging on that cross He knows Himself kinsman with those who are reddening their hands with the blood of the Representative of God and bringing judgment upon their and His people. He is the conscience of these, His less conscientious brothers. He realizes, as they do not, the enormity of what they are doing, and He foresees the dire sequel which must come in this moral universe, where what is sown is reaped. With a prophet's certainty He sees devastation and slaughter overtaking the men, women and children He fain would save for God. His conscience makes His own the guilt of those who were crucifying Him. They knew not the things which belonged to their peace, but He knew the catastrophe that would result from their blindness. They knew not what they were now doing in slaying Him. And His sympathy with them in their ignorance, plunged His soul into midnight blackness.

> "I felt," wrote John Woolman in his Journal, "the depth and extent of the misery of my fellow-creatures, separated from the Divine harmony, and it was greater than I could bear, and I was crushed down under it."

From the lowest abyss which any of His followers have plumbed, we peer down further still into that dark deep

47

in which Jesus felt Himself bereft of God, and from which He cried: "Forsaken!"

But, oh, how grateful we must be that the Son of God went down into this awful gulf, as deep and deeper than any of us are ever taken! In our blackest doubts and in our most baffling moral confusions, when that woesome word is on our lips: "Why? Why? Why?" we are sure that He understands our bewilderment, our sense of God-forsakenness.

❧ WHEN OUR "WHY?" IS ANSWERED

Words spoken to God are immeasurably above words spoken about Him. There is a huge difference between saying: "Why hast Thou?" and "Why has He?" If we cannot understand God's dealings, if we resent His will, if we smart under a sense of His injustice, the test of our faith is whether we tell someone else about it, or go straight to Him with our inquiry: "My God, why?" It is then that God has His chance; He cannot explain Himself to the man who keeps away from Him.

Our sufferings strengthen our faith provided that in them we set ourselves to go straight to God with our questions. A storm that nearly wrecks a vessel may carry it into port if the ship keeps headed in the direction of its haven. The winds themselves drive it homeward. An experience that threatens to overwhelm faith sweeps the life Godward, if the soul addresses itself to Him: "My God." When a man really wants to get at His Father in heaven,

> *the hardest pang whereon*
> *He lays his mutinous head may be a Jacob's stone.*

The trust of Jesus on the cross formed the ladder down which the loving comradeship of His Father ran to meet Him. He emerged from the darkness of death perfected, as the Author and Finisher of faith.

And the clear-seeing men of the New Testament give us one more answer to the question: "Why?" when they quote the words of the prophet: "By His stripes we are healed." Suppose the prayer in Gethsemane that this cup might be taken from Him had been granted; suppose that instead of the arrest and trial some of the leaders in Jerusalem had come to Jesus' rescue; and after a few months in which the excitement died down, suppose the Sanhedrin had altered its decision, and Jesus had quietly retired to Galilee and lived on to a hale old age surrounded by faithful disciples, more and more esteemed by a once indifferent or hostile public, and had passed by a peaceful and painless death home to God; what would have been the effect of His life, and what the measure of His influence in the world? We should have called Him wisest of sages, and brightest of earth's luminous characters; but would we have adored Him as Redeemer of the world?

It is easy to protest against vicarious suffering. Why should He, or you or I, or any other, suffer for others? My God, why? There is no answer from God or from man save that it seems to be in the structure and fabric of things. Life is born through another's pangs; liberty is achieved for nations through the blood of those who themselves never enjoy the hard-won freedom. One soweth and another reapeth. It is so in literature, in art, in invention, in discovery, in faith. The pioneers are not the possessors; the explorers are rarely the dwellers in the land; the sowers are not often the harvesters. And the sowing has usually to be in tears. Possibly the seed would not otherwise be watered, or the ground softened with moisture. It is part of the scheme of things: "Where pain ends, gain ends, too."

But that may only put more persistence into our query: "My God, why?" God, the Lord of heaven and earth, cannot be relieved of responsibility for the scheme of things. Why has He made it so? To that there is no reply; or at all events none that we can understand. But when men go in faith directly to Him, they make this amazing discovery that He is Himself sharing the very suffering at which they rebel. God's own sowing has been in tears. If the sons of God shouted for joy when the foundations of the earth were laid, the Creator Himself was straining in effort and burdened with a heavy sense of His obligation. And all through the ages He has carried His children and felt their pains as His own. Did some vision of His Father's own pain come to the soul of the Son of God when He appealed "My God, why?" And if His question had no clear answer, any more than yours or mine, was the amazing glimpse of the suffering Father of all so wondrous and so satisfying with its assurance of fellowship that questioning ceased and trustful companionship took its place? "Father, into Thy hands I commend My spirit."

For if God Himself sows in tears, and yet is God the Lord, whose purpose must eventually prevail, the anguished children of men know that their pain and crying are not barren. The Son who asks the question, "My God, why?" and still hangs in the black darkness that lay over the earth, has been coming again ever since, heavily burdened, but now with an ever-increasing load of golden sheaves. Other sons and daughters to whom His cup is given know now that their bitter experiences have a redemptive power. In their measure they are filling up the deficit of their Lord's sufferings. And to them, as to Him, and as also to His and their God, to whom the hard question of pain is put: "My God, why?" It is granted sometimes now in part and in the fulness of time more clearly to see of the travail of their souls, and be satisfied.

ᴥᶚ WHAT IS OUR ULTIMATE DEPENDENCE?

Leigh Hunt, speaking of Napoleon's final weeks when he escaped from Elba and made his stand at Waterloo, wrote: "No great principle stood by him." He was taking a chance —the chance of rallying France's forces, and by a bold military stroke destroying the as-yet-separated allied armies. He lost. A spiritual imponderable was wanting: "No great principle stood by him."

Jesus' journey to Jerusalem appears a similar desperate venture. He was taking the chance of winning the Passover pilgrims, of appealing to the rulers of the nation, of being welcomed at the capital. He can have been under no illusions as to what His reception would be. He was taking the all-but-certain chance of being assassinated or executed. Very well, if so, He believed His death would accomplish what His life had meagrely begun. A great principle was standing by Him—Love which beareth, believeth, hopeth, endureth all and never faileth. That had been His principle all along. He was its embodiment now.

And the result?

> And e'er His agony was done
> Before the westering sun went down,
> Crowning that day with crimson crown,
> He knew
> That He had won.

That is poetic conjecture. What passed in Jesus' mind that dark day we cannot say. He died; and His body was laid in a grave. But from His cross consequences have never ceased to ensue. It has been the constant disquieter of consciences, forcing men to search themselves and to scrutinise the life about them and the society of which they are part. It has been the spur pressing them to do differently and to alter human relations to accord with His mind. It has been a power—a mighty and lasting force—strengthening men against their own inclinations and reluctances, and enabling them all down the centuries to attempt and (in some measure) compass things akin in quality to this Crucified.

Yes, Jesus was not gambling; He was hazarding Himself on that of which He knew. A great principle stood by Him. Why? What explanation is there so reasonable as His own —love that suffers with and for others to redeem them is the nature of Him who is over all and through all and in all— God blessed forever.

ஒ THE LORD OF HISTORY

We live in a day when more people the earth over have a vivid sense of being in history—encompassed by forces which affect them for weal or for appalling woe. We can appreciate One who took the uncontrollable factors of the world of His day—took them in their fell fury in His torn hands and feet and pierced side, took them on His conscience, the just for the unjust, took them in their bewildering darkness on His mind; and so took them in steadfast faith, despite the clutch of doubt and despair, that for millions He is the Lord of history, men's most potent Contemporary age after age. They look up through the welter of baffling events in quiet confidence, and behind and over them they keep their eyes fixed on "the throne of God and of the Lamb."

ஒ WHAT THE CRUCIFIED ACCOMPLISHED

When one thinks of Christ in the light of all that His life and death have wrought through the centuries for the transformation and ennoblement of our race, one remembers that at the core of our puzzling universe there is That which is capable of producing Him, and working in and with Him. And when we ask what That is, no explanation seems to serve but his own—a God of love, akin to Himself. From such a Father he comes; He makes His forgiveness felt redeemingly.

He takes away the barrier sinful men feel between themselves and a holy God. It is not that the death of Jesus alters God's attitude towards His rebellious children. It is God Himself who sends His Son, who comes to us in His Son, and in Him takes our sin and carries our shame.

In the National Gallery in London there is a painting in which one sees Christ on the cross against a black background. Darkness wraps Him in loneliness and apparent God-abandonment. He, and He alone, loves men enough to suffer and die for us. The universe is uncaring. But if one looks at that canvas intently, there emerges from the blackness the dim outline of another crucified Sufferer—the Father sharing Golgotha with His Son. "God was in Christ reconciling the world unto Himself"; "God commendeth His own love towards us." In taking on Himself the confusion and doubt of a sinful world, Christ took away the shrouding darkness sufficiently to let a Father's face shine through. On that cruel cross where the combination of the forces which bedevil every human society and every man's own heart brought Jesus of Nazareth to a death of agony and shame, He did most in those brief hours to set afoot counter forces which down the ages continue to defeat them. The strongest preventive of our living selfishly and arrogantly is that haunting Figure at Golgotha. The mightiest incentive to our taking on our consciences the wrongs and injustices of our world and spending ourselves to amend them is that seemingly defeated and frustrated Victim of His social situation.

✃ THE CROSS WAS NOT THE END

The crucifixion is not the final scene in our Gospels, nor does it stand on the pages of history without a glorious sequel. The enemies of Jesus were sure that they had given Him and His cause a quietus. He was banished from their earth, done for, and would never again disturb Jerusalem or the Roman Empire. His friends gave Him up: all they had hoped for was irretrievably lost. He Himself in that bleak moment felt deserted. Crying into the dark, and listening, there was no whisper in reply.

But the answer came, and it keeps coming. It is coming today from innumerable souls who find themselves strengthened as they take from Him the believing words: "My God, My God." They are going through their conflicts with a courage which comes from His cross. They are being lifted out of their doubt by His steadfast faith. "In that He Himself hath suffered, being tempted, He is able to succor them that are tempted." He is able to save unto the uttermost all of us who from the bottommost depths of our bafflement and our need come unto God through Him.

✃ THROUGH TRAGEDY TO GLORY

In the bitter wars of the seventeenth century, a son of the Duke of Ormonde gallantly laid down his life in what he and his father believed the cause of justice. Someone commiserated the older man on his sore loss. The Duke replied:

> I would not give my dead son for the best living
> son in Christendom.

Yes, life is tragic—never more so than in our time. And the outcome of this tragedy is not yet plain, nor likely to become discernible in any near future. But it is through tragedy that men attain greatness of character—and that clearly is a chief end of our schooling here. The best of our race was "made perfect through suffering." And it is through tragedy that men achieve ends for which genera- tions rise up and call them blessed. Why this or that par- ticular tragedy is necessary in God's purposes, and why good and evil are so inextricably intermixed in His re- sponses to prayers, none can presume to guess. It remains forever true that to our sight (as an ancient poet put it) God's way is in the sea and His paths in the deep waters and His footsteps are not known. But those who, following His beloved Son, make their choices in prayer, discover themselves led by a way that they know not to a destination where they see of the travail of their souls and are satisfied.

ON OUR BEHALF

There are two words associated with Jesus in His suffer- ing on Calvary. One is the word "substitute." He did this in our place for us. The other is the word "exemplar." He did it that we might also do it. And I think both are true and you do not get an adequate view of the Cross of Christ unless you take both into your thought.

A substitute. Here is a mountain with a tangled forest on its slopes; and an adventurous soul comes along and blazes a trail up that mountain, slips over the rocks, loses himself in the bogs, finds himself tangled in the underbrush, but on, on, on, on he goes, until he gets to the sunlit summit. He is the pioneer. There is a magnificent phrase applied by Peter to Jesus Christ which ought to be translated by just that word "pioneer." Our version translates it, "the Prince of Life." The Revised Version has it in the margin, "the Author of Life." But a far better word is "the Pioneer of Life." He saw the track toward God up yonder, and He saw man down here in the iniquities and injustices and inhumanities of that life that He knew so well, that He had tasted the bitterness and force of, and through doubts and struggles He became "the Pioneer of Faith," as the author of the Epistle to the Hebrews calls Him. He found the new and living way up through His suffering, His flesh, into oneness with the heart of God. And He did it that no man ever need repeat His experience. He did it for us, for all mankind, our Substitute. You only need to have one pathfinder, one trailmaker. And what He suffered no one knows until he tries to appreciate the mental anguish of Jesus in Gethsemane casting about for some possible way out other than the way of that cross. "O my Father, if, if it be possible,"—our Substitute.

And our Exemplar. Our acceptance of the sacrifice of Christ means that we take just that same cross for ourselves. It cannot be escaped. "I fill up on my part that which is lacking," says Saint Paul, "the deficit in the sufferings of Christ for His body's sake, His Church." Beloved, if God so loved, we ought also. Yes, as we dedicate ourselves to bring in the Kingdom of God on the earth we must expect in our measure and according to the fashion of our day just such opposition, even unto death perhaps for some of us. We must take upon our conscience the iniquities, the unbrotherliness, the ungodliness of our world, and feel them as a crushing load, even as they crushed the spirit and conscience of the Son of God; and in sympathy with the whole family of mankind we must be willing to share with them all that they undergo, if we would be in fellowship with Him. "If any man will come after me, let him deny himself and take up his cross and follow me."

There is the fellowship of the sufferings in every age. Are you going to be in it? The vicariously suffering Father revealed in the vicariously suffering Son, our Savior and

Elder Brother, followed by a company animated and dominated by the spirit of love, the redemptive Spirit. Is that the fellowship where you and I want to be? Dare we be in any other fellowship? Could we be satisfied in any other fellowship?

✒§ SEEKING THE MEANING OF THE CROSS

Calvary still remains a place of discovery. Who will begin to list what men and women find out there? No man looks thoughtfully at the Crucified without discovering something hideously disagreeable about himself. His own motives and impulses are so terribly like the factors which enacted that tragedy. The cross always makes us feel ashamed of ourselves. And no man can look thoughtfully at the Crucified without discovering something all but irresistibly appealing in the Life embodied there. What he wishes he might become, what he longs to achieve, is there. There is the life upon which he knows that he turns his back time after time, but which haunts him and casts its spell over him. He knows himself as he does not like to know himself, and he knows another self which he wishes he might know as himself. But that is about as far as his knowledge will go, so long as he only *thinks* about the cross.

Should he, however, yield to the fascination of the Crucified, should he actually begin to walk in the way of that Son of man, discovery after discovery will open up before him. He will become acquainted with grief—grief at the injustices and thoughtlessness that mar earth's brotherhood, grief at the irresponsibility, the prejudices, the distrust, that keep men apart and embitter life, grief at the self-seeking and unbelief which hold men far from God. He will become acquainted with joy—joy in the sense of being used, even to the extent of being wellnigh used up, joy in the zest of battle for righteousness, joy in the unexpected comradeships which come to him by the way—for the path is by no means entirely solitary;—there is a fellowship of companions of the Son of man who once trod His way alone. He will become acquainted with wisdom—the wisdom of the silence that does not answer back, the wisdom of the sympathy which seeks to feel what others feel before it does anything with or for them, the wisdom of the love that beareth, believeth, hopeth, endureth all and never faileth. He will become acquainted with power—the mysterious feeling of reinforcement that comes to us when we devote ourselves to the highest we can think of, the endurance which seems given from some unknown source of supply to those who bring themselves to bear the apparently intolerable, the force which its possessors scarcely are aware of, but which others recognise and respond to, that is theirs who spend and are spent for the uncaring and the unlovely. And when a man becomes acquainted with such grief and joy and wisdom and power, is there anything deeper or higher, finer or mightier, in the universe for him to know? Are not such grief and joy and wisdom and power the qualities, the very nature of Him whom Jesus adored as God, the Lord of heaven and earth? To be acquainted with, to be friends with, such grief, such joy, such wisdom, such power, is to be acquainted with the Most High, to be friends with the Father in heaven. This is to know God; and this is the discovery of those who share the cross.

To know God—what a presumptuous statement! In what sense is it possible? Knowledge of anything depends upon some fitness in us to the object to be known. The same vibrations of ether are to the skin heat, and to the eye light. The same vibrations of the air are to the body an imperceptible tremor and to the ear sound. We have to develop the organ which equips us to interpret anything and to understand it. And this is emphatically so of our knowledge of persons. An English critic some years ago said: "To understand some writers we must change our planet and wait patiently till we are acclimatized." Great authors as a rule have to educate a public to appreciate them, and often they wait years, perhaps until they themselves are dead, to be prized and understood. We can all think of books that meant nothing to us once. We wondered why anyone praised them. But we have since grown up to them, and have come back to them with eagerness. Life's experiences have developed in us the capacities to interpret what was once lost upon us. It is often said that no hero is a hero to his valet. That is not because the hero is no hero, but because the valet is a valet. Some fitness, some affinity, is essential to appreciation. In one of the most vivid accounts of the persecutions of the early Church, there is a description of the scene when Pothinus, the leader of the Christians at Lyons and Vienne in Gaul, an old saint of ninety years, was dragged by the soldiers before the magistrates. In the course of the examination the governor asked Pothinus who was the God of the Christians. And the old man replied: "If thou art worthy, thou shalt know."

PRAYERS

O God, Lord of earth and heaven, Thou art great beyond our thought, and Thou art love high above our frail and faulty hearts. We adore Thee manifest in Thy Son crucified for us and for the whole family of Thy sinning children. Always Thou hast been afflicted in our afflictions, and shamed in our evil; and always Thou hast given Thyself to lift us to be companions of Thy mind. Thou knowest all things; Thou knowest that we love Thee. Yet our hearts condemn us, and number us among those who deny and betray and crucify love. But Thou art greater than our

59

hearts. By Thy love in Christ, who bearest our sins and forgivest us, redeem us to share His faith and courage, yea His readiness to dare all in love, that the world of our day may be freed from selfishness and injustice and unbelief, and men everywhere be one in Thee, through Christ, the Saviour of us all.

O God who lovest with an everlasting love, and from old hast been afflicted in all Thy children's affliction, bearing them in Thy pity and redeeming them, Thou hast made Thy Word flesh in Jesus, and hast bared Thy heart to us in His cross.

We stand before it, burdened. Lo! this is our world: it slays its best; yea, it is enmity against thee, its God. And these who condemn and crucify Him, are our kinsmen— mind of our mind, spirit of our spirit, Who shall deliver us?

We stand before it amazed. Behold how He loved us! We cannot escape His constraint. We can no longer live unto ourselves.

We stand before it dedicated. Such love is not for us alone, but for a whole world. We dare not keep for ourselves what belongs to our brethren everywhere. Good Shepherd, Thou hast other sheep; them also Thou must bring. And how shall they hear Thy voice except Thy disciples become Thy word for them? We offer ourselves a living sacrifice to fill up on our part that which is lacking in the sufferings of Christ for His Body's sake, the Church.

O Saviour of the world, uplifted that Thou mightest draw all men unto Thee, we bring Thee in tender intercession those who are in pain or sorrow or loneliness, and especially such as are self-imprisoned. Let the heart of God unveiled at Calvary be their comfort and their deliverer. And grant that they and we, and all who have looked upon

Thee in Thy passion, may bear the marks of Thy cross upon us, and live in that love which believeth, hopeth, endureth all and never faileth.

Gracious Father, who in the life and teaching of Thy Son hast shown us the true way of blessedness, Thou hast also shown us in His sufferings and death that the path of duty may lead to the cross and the reward of faithfulness may be a crown of thorns. Grant us grace early to learn these harder lessons. May we become companions of His conscience who felt as His own the sins of His brethren, and comrades of His sacrifice who counted not His life too dear to offer for their redemption. And grant that knowing the fellowship of His suffering we may also know the power of His resurrection, and be more than conquerors through Thy love in him, our Saviour Jesus Christ.

O God, who hast shown us in the victory of Thy Son, Jesus Christ, that all things work together for good unto them that love, help us to know that whatever accords with the Spirit of Christ shares His unconquerable power. May we bring in thought to His empty tomb the truth that is blocked by ignorance or prejudice, the justice that is thwarted by greed or selfishness, the faith that seems denied by adverse facts, the love that is slain by bitterness or indifference, and know that these shall surely triumph. Enable us to bring our own purposes of good that have miscarried, the ideals we seem incapable of making actual, the efforts of our love that have failed, the faith whose mountain is still unremoved, and tell our hearts again that all these are not in vain in the Lord.

Lord God of the living unto whom all live, while we keep the festival of our Saviour's abiding life in Thee we remember with thanksgiving all who have dwelt in love and so dwell forever in Thee. Strengthen us with the confidence that they who were bound up with us and made a dear part of being cannot be lost; that the powers in them we would have helped to bring out and the powers in us they would have brought to light are still unfolding in them and in us. Comfort those whose thoughts when they recall the grave of Jesus fly off to graves where their own beloved have been laid. May they meet Thee, who art Lord of all worlds as well as of ours, and know that in meeting Thee they are truly met by those who live with Thee forevermore.

The Power of the Resurrection

A second-century Christian, writing to his friend Diognetus, characterizes Christianity as "this new interest which
has entered into life." We look upon each day with a fresh
expectancy; we view ourselves with a new reverence. The
waste wilderness within from which we despaired of producing anything must under Christ's recreating touch become an Eden, where we feel

> *Pison and Euphrates roll*
> *Round the great garden of a kingly soul.*

But is this emparadised life to be some day thrown aside?
J. Romanes, whose Christian upbringing had instilled in
him the distinctively Christian appreciation of the value
of his own life, when his scientific opinions robbed him of
the hope of immortality, wrote: "Although from henceforth the precept 'to work while it is day' will doubtless
but gain an intensified force from the terribly intensified
meaning of the words that 'the night cometh when no man
can work,' yet when at times I think, as think at times I
must, of the appalling contrast between the hallowed glory
of that creed which once was mine, and the lonely mystery
of existence as I now find it, at such times I shall ever feel
it impossible to avoid the sharpest pang of which my instinct is susceptible."

Jesus came that life might become more abundant, and
every human relation deeper, tenderer, richer. It is to love
that death is intolerable. Professor Palmer of Harvard once
delivered a lecture upon *"Intimations of Immortality in
the Sonnets of Shakespeare,"* in which he showed that when
a man finds himself truly in love mortality becomes unthinkable to him. And for Christians love and friendship contain
more than they do for other men. Christ takes us more
completely out of ourselves and wraps us up in those to

65

whom we feel ourselves bound. He makes life touch at more points, life draw from life more copious inspirations, life cling to life with more affectionate tenacity. He roots and grounds us in love, and that is to root us in the souls of other men; then to tear them from us irrevocably—parents, children, husband, wife, lover, beloved, friend—is to leave us of all men most pitiable.

Love—the prisoned God in man—is in the universe itself which sends them on through the years conquering and to conquer. That demonstration in history confirms Jesus' trust in God, sets a public seal which the whole world can see to the correctness of His testimony to Him whom He found in the unseen and in whose cause He laid down His life.

And Jesus has made another contribution to the answer of our question: it is through Him that we form our pictures of the life to which we look forward so certainly. The New Testament expectations centre about Jesus Himself: "With Me in paradise"; "Where I am, there also shall My servant be"; "I go to prepare a place for you"; "So shall we ever be with the Lord." Men who had experienced Christ's hold upon them through all the divisive circumstances of life had no doubt of His continuing grasp upon them through death; they spoke of the Christian dead as "the dead in Christ"—the dead under His transforming control. Neither death nor life could separate them from His love.

Since we see God, the Lord of heaven, in Jesus, the only and all-satisfying knowledge we have of the future life is that it will accord with the will of the Father of Jesus Christ. Of its details we can merely say: "Eye hath not seen, nor ear heard, neither have entered into the heart of man, the things which God hath prepared for them that love Him." But we know God in Christ; we are certain of many things that cannot be included in a life where

66

His heart has its way; the city of our hopes has walls; but it also has gates on every side, and we are certain of its hospitality to all that accords with the mind of Christ. That which renders the life within the veil not all dark to us as yet is the fact that "the Lamb is the light thereof." There is a connection between it and our life today; the one Lord rules earth and heaven; and Him we know through Jesus. Humbly acknowledging that we know but in part, glad that the future has in store for us glorious surprises, we are convinced that for us there waits a life in God in which His children shall attain their Christlike selves in Christlike fellowship one with another and with Him, their Christlike Father. More than this who cares to know? More than this, for what can Christians wish?

THE GOOD THAT CANNOT DIE

Shortly before the death of Mr. William Howard Taft, I was strolling with him in Washington and ventured to ask him what he thought of the prospects of the League of Nations, then patently feeble and seemingly collapsing. He stopped abruptly, squared round to face me, and said:

> You ought to know that in this world the best things get crucified; *but they rise again.*

That was St. Paul's conviction of what occurs in history on the lips of a modern Christian statesman. Toilers for fellowship—fellowship among nations, among races, among the uneasily adjusted groups of human beings—may look back to that mighty act, and then look in on their resources and look out on the contemporary scene sure of invisible factors working with them. We have at hand "the exceeding greatness of His power to usward who believe, according to the working of the strength of His might which He wrought

67

in Christ, when He raised Him from the dead." Courage then! This is the measure of the force at work in and with us for fellowship.

But no attempt to give the Bible's view of history dare ignore the perspective in which that history is set. Its goal is not in history, but beyond it. God's mighty acts in the centuries have their culmination outside the centuries.

Thomas Carlyle wrote:

> In the wondrous, boundless jostle of things (an aimful Power presiding over it, say rather dwelling in it) a result comes out that may be put up with.

That surely is a very moderate expectation. We can say that at times results come out which set whole people jubilating. What small beginnings the Christian Church had, even if God worked in and with her according to the strength of such might! And how chequered her history from the start to this hour! Christians early learned not to look for the completion of their hopes at any time on earth. They remained (in words which our generation had dropped from its vocabulary) "pilgrims and strangers" moving towards a better country where God's purposes arrive.

An older Carlyle declared:

> Eternity is my one strong city. I look into it fixedly now and then. . . . The universe is full of love, but also of inexorable sternness and severity, and it remains forever true that God reigns. Patience! Silence! Hope!

We have lost much in blotting the eternal prospect from our horizon and confining our attention to this one world. Men with both in mind see events in a truer perspective. They put up with delays less fretfully. They cherish modest anticipations of what can be accomplished in human affairs.

When the city of their ideal is not within reach, they do not decline to move towards some suburb of it which may be accessible. While they work hard to improve that suburb, and open it to all the influences of the city of God, they do not confuse arrangements which man creates, makeshift arrangements, even the best and wisest of them, with the city whose builder and maker is God.

Nor do men whose ultimate hope is anchored "within the veil" let that be an opiate, dulling them to wrongs which should be righted or contenting them with suburban communities which need complete making over to approximate the heavenly city in whose neighborhood they belong. The living God whose will is fully achieved Yonder is working mightily here "in the midst of the years," and believing men can be counted on to deal lusty blows for righteousness at His side. Others may become disillusioned and cynical; not they. One never hears them saying: "It is too good to be true." If something which they had hoped for is not accomplished, they admit that it was not yet good enough to be true. They do not expect mankind to find itself settling in a promised land. Throughout history mankind must continue on the march. But they are confident of a heavenly commonwealth, into which shall be brought the honor and the glory of the nations; and the life of that commonwealth moves serenely in light from One who in history was slain.

✑§ THE GOD OF OUR GREATEST HOPE

You recall Pompilia's final word about her husband, the brutal Guido who had abused her with every devilish ingenuity:

> *We shall not meet in this world or the next;*
> *But where will God be absent? In His face*

69

> *Is light, but in His shadow healing too:*
> *Let Guido touch the shadow and be healed.*

That is the God of hope.

Consider the universal fact of death. If a man entertains very moderate expectations for himself and for his fellow-mortals, these may be reached in the seventy or eighty years which are at present the most we can count on for earthly existence. But if we once begin to long that we and our brothers may become full-statured in wisdom and sympathy and devotion—how unlikely are any to reach the goal! We cannot put a university course in character-discipline into a primary grade where ethical infants like ourselves are learning to appreciate our world and to live together helpfully in it. You remember Professor William James' answer to the question: "Why do you believe in personal immortality?" "Because I am just getting fit to live," and Mr. James was sixty-two when he wrote that.

And, explain it as you will, life knits us into dear comradeships with other human beings and makes us mean so much to each other that, when death takes one, the survivor's heart is fairly ripped to pieces. In such experiences the most unbelieving become passionately wistful. Men may resign themselves to regard these partings as final, and say of friend or parent or child or wife: "We shall never see each other again." But let us make plain the contrast of a different conviction. In his autobiography, shortly after his wife's death, Richard Baxter writes:

> I am waiting to be met: the door is open: death
> will quickly draw the veil, and make us see how
> near we were to God and one another and did
> not sufficiently know it.

Those who live and work with Jesus come to share both His insights into human beings and His insights into the universe. And they believe in the God of hope. They risk their all on the supposition that Jesus knew. Again and again in their restricted range of experience they discover Him most wise. They are ready to trust His wisdom in matters beyond their present power to test.

Edward Fitzgerald, the translator and in part creator of the cynical quatrains of *Omar Khayyam,* once listened in a chapel at Bedford to a Good Friday sermon, which he admitted "shook his soul," and wrote in a letter:

> Oh this wonderful, wonderful world, and we who stand in the middle of it are in a maze, except poor Matthew of Bedford, who fixes his eyes upon a wooden Cross and has no misgivings whatsoever.

Life, as such men see it, opens up surprising and gladdening resources. Fitzgerald tells how he found this minister making poor folk spiritually millionaires. "I was quite overset," he confesses.

And for those thus enriched only one explanation is convincing. Jesus was not deluded, and He does not delude. The universe contains and brings forth the good things of which He is so sure—faith and hope and love. And His believed-in and hoped-for good things come to pass and become the most valuable possessions of men and of human society because His fundamental conviction is true. "I thank Thee, Father, Lord of heaven and earth." He is the God of hope.

WHEN LIFE IS LOST AND WON

It is not a question whether Jesus survived death, and continues to live somewhere today. If love be not the foundation of the universe, would He have wished to go on living? Could His dearest friends wish to doom Him to exist in a universe forever at variance with His spirit, to dwell in worlds always uncongenial to His nature, to repeat time and again Gethsemane and Calvary, unless broken and exhausted, He gives up trying, and ceases to be the Jesus we love and adore? Nor is it a question of how He rose from the dead, or with what body He resumed intercourse with His disciples, or whether this or that particular in the narrative of the resurrection in the Gospels is historically accurate. These are details. The question is whether the crucifixion ended Jesus' career in our world and deprived Him of further power to affect its life. The indisputable Easter fact, however you choose to explain it, is that Jesus was a more potent factor in Jerusalem in the weeks and months after His death on Calvary than when He rode into the city amid the crowds or sat with His disciples in the Upper Room. Nor does our evidence lie in the past merely. Jesus remains a living Force in the world of our day—our most influential Contemporary.

John Drinkwater has written:

> Shakespeare is dust, and will not come
> To question from his Avon tomb,
> And Socrates and Shelley keep
> An Attic and Italian sleep.
>
> They will not see us, nor again
> Shall indignation light the brain
> Where Lincoln on his woodland height
> Tells out the spring and winter night.
>
> They see not. But, O Christians, who
> Throng Holborn and Fifth Avenue,
> May you not meet, in spite of death,
> A traveller from Nazareth?[2]

[2] Reprinted by permission of Samuel French, Ltd. Copyright (c) 1922 by John Drinkwater.

✑ THIS LIFE'S INSUFFICIENCY

In these three score and ten years, longer or shorter, who of us succeeds in more than commencing to share His Father's purpose, commencing to be sympathetic, responsive and responsible, commencing to enter on life with God? And the commencement is so enriching that we cry out to go on. Men and women who do not interpret life as Jesus did, who have no interest in His God and His plans, no longing to see His hopes fulfilled, no passionate attachment to Him, may conceivably content themselves with what earth offers them. But even they, as we well know, will have moments when friendship seems too big a thing to be explored in any period of mortal years, moments when vision fascinates them with a prospect of a kindlier world too different from ours to be expected within their lifetime and too captivating not to fill them with an eagerness to share in it, moments when love opens up for them a height, breadth, length and depth in some other soul and in their own which makes them feel they were not meant to die. And when beside these natural human experiences we enter into Jesus' friendship for men, into His vision of the world that should be, into His experience of the love of God, then it is impossible for us to content ourselves with earth's brief term, and such confinement becomes unthinkable. These cravings of our natures are their adaptation to our eternal Father; this prayer to be saved from death is the response of our spirits to His will that we should share with Him His ageless life.

Unless one cares for the Father whom Jesus revealed, unless one shares His interests and likes the purpose on which His heart is set, Easter must be anything but a happy festival. Its victory of long ago declares so unmistakably who rules the world and who succeeds in His world—not expedient Pilates, not men who put property-rights in temple courts above the human need of a homelike Father's house for all peoples, not traders engrossed in profiting in sheep and financial exchange without concern whether the souls of their brothers are enriched in God, not traditionally devout people with minds closed to unconventional ideas of God and duty, not a disloyal friend. Easter affirms a universe into which Jesus fits, a spiritual world corresponding to His character—a universe in which plans discordant with His aims, motives offensive to His conscience, lives at variance with His love, are inevitably thwarted and fail. It gives assurance of victorious life to those, and those only, who are in harmony with the purpose of His God. "Love never faileth," and everything unloving surely dies. On the same night in which Jesus prayed to be saved from death, He said of another, "Good were it for that man if he had not been born"—he does not belong in God's world. The same men who on Easter found Jesus risen into triumphant life spoke of Judas Iscariot as gone "to his own place." Oh, men and women, are we fit to live, fit to live with God in earth or heaven, fit to be companionable sons and daughters of Him whose mind and heart and conscience, as Easter witnesses, accord with Jesus Christ?

৺§ THE CRUCIFIED AND LIVING LORD

Jesus was not concerned mainly with His own survival and continuing existence somewhere in the universe. Few folk in His day questioned that. But He had set Himself to establish God's reign, and how could He be sure that He would go on doing that despite death and burial? His one aim had been to find God's will for Him and to do or bear it. Gethsemane was His preparation for the only immortality which He coveted. The prayer at Golgotha,

"Father into Thy hands I commend my spirit," was His making sure that God in His own wise way would hold fast and continue to employ Him. Easter and all in which He has had part since is the vindication of His trust. He made the going on of His cause and His own going on sure in God.

There is something egotistical in worrying over our own survival, as though we were indispensable to the universe. But if, like Christ, we lose ourselves in God's purpose, and live and labor and are ready to die that His will be achieved, we place ourselves at His disposal. There is no egotism in that. We make no claim where or how we be employed. We trust our all to God and God is faithful to the trust. Our labor, as Paul put it with Christ's resurrection before Him, is not in vain in the Lord. Faulty, mistaken, needing in our case pardon and correction, still He keeps it part of His world's unalterable good. And as for ourselves, He is never done with us. In partnership with Him for our brief mortal years, He does not scrap sons and daughters, like worn-out tools. A Jesus has His unique future—His age-long life as the Saviour and Leader of untold brethren. And we, His imperfect followers, too, know a Father's faithfulness. All that we have tried to do for Him, and all that we are in ourselves, we commit to His hands. Sure of Him, what other assurance do we need?

◁§ BEYOND EARTH-CENTREDNESS

The last few generations have been earth-centred. But time, even if one looks ahead many millenia on this planet, hems us in a too-confining horizon. God is from everlasting to everlasting, and our life and destiny are with Him. Were earth to become a far happier and friendlier globe, it would still be man's dwelling for a span of years only, and although that span for the average man may be prolonged by some decades, here have we no continuing city. And the best things earth can give us, schooling in thoughtfulness, in patience, in courage, in love, in trust—hearts with inclusive sympathies, consciences sensitive to obligation, tastes for things just, pure, lovely, minds hospitable to truth, spirits companionable with God—these we cannot hand on to successors; these are personal acquisitions; these become ourselves. These we take with us and continue to advance in with God.

It is in Him and in Him only that the fulfillments of the abiding desires of souls can be looked for. What that corporate life with Him will be for those who pass to it among the peoples who bring in the glory of the nations, what that commonwealth in which spirits meet who dwelt here centuries apart in the generations of human history, what that fellowship where those *shall rejoin one another* who walked together for brief stretches on earth, linked in interests and knit in dear affections, we do not know. Enough if in part we know God. "The Lord is my chosen portion and my cup; thou holdest my lot."

> *To an open house in the evening,*
> *Home shall men come.*
> *To an older place than Eden,*
> *To a taller town than Rome,*
> *To the end of the way of the wandering star,*
> *To the things that cannot be and that are.*

◆§ MORE THAN CONQUERORS

Some years ago when a gallant figure in British public affairs died with his career scarcely begun, Katherine Tynan wrote:

Whither goest, adventurer?
With the East upon thine eyes,
Stepping with the old blithesome air
On the last splendid enterprise;
Who hast heard the piper play
Over the hills and far away.

It is the fashion of the hour to decry the longing for ever-lasting life as selfish: "Why set such store by your wretched self as to suppose that you ought to be kept living forever and ever? Are not three-score and ten years, more or less, quite enough of you for the universe?" Yes, and more than enough if we are doomed to remain as we are and repeat the futilities and follies of our yesterdays. But is there anything selfish, or hurtful to the social weal, in Jesus' continuing to live on—the factor that He has been in our earth these nineteen centuries and the Light of a more glorious commonwealth within the veil?

The Christian hope is not that souls, because inherently they are everlasting, shall continue to exist; our hope is that because God's fellowship has no limit or end, the worst who yields to Him shall grow into His likeness, and the faithful with Him shall bring to pass His plans for His children. The mysterious venture on which God embarked when He evolved sons and daughters capable of becoming His comrades, He is not going to abandon. The hazard He took when He stooped to be the Friend of such unlikely folk as you and me, He still has the courage to continue. The dream to which He devoted Himself of a society of just men made perfect in the stature of Christ is His eternal purpose. He will not fail nor be discouraged until it be achieved. It has cost Him Calvary—untold Calvaries—but He fainteth not. Easter is the festival of His dependableness—"that your faith and hope might be in God."

On what do we depend?—that discloses our religion. Do

we rely on luck? on ourselves? on some power that we can annex to our purposes? Or do we depend utterly on such love as that to which Jesus prayed: "Father, into Thy hands I commend." Here is the world of our time with its heart-aching problems—unemployment, poverty, racial discrimi-nations, national pride and greed. These demand all the wisdom clear-seeing minds can offer—and something more. Here are those for whom we are personally responsible with their kinks and twists, and here are we with our flaws and frailties of thought and feeling and conscience. They and we need the discipline of life and the skilled handling of the wisest whom Providence can supply—and still something more. Here is death, the resistless divider, sundering the most devoted hearts and ending the most useful careers. Only the God of love on whom Jesus de-pended is sufficient for these things. Those who have known Him speak of victory plus—they know themselves to be "more than conquerors." Neither death nor life, things present nor things to come, height nor depth can separate from Him. And over the hills and far away the trusting go on love's endlessly inventive adventures, confident in Him who is able to do exceeding abundantly above all that they ask or think.

ᴈᔓ WHEN THE MORNING DAWNS

Some time ago there was published a brief memorial collection of the fugitive writings of a young man of letters who had died on the threshhold of his career. It is intro-duced by William Rose Benet, who writes: "We have all had such friends, mysteriously—stupidly—one felt—taken before they had been given time to leave some permanent impress of themselves except in our hearts. I cannot, for myself, believe that a spirit, such as his, is wasted. . . . I myself believe in a reason and a purpose for such spirits which does not exhaust itself merely upon this imperfect world. It is this faith, largely, that helps me to live."

Call our loftiest hopes of the life-to-come illusions; that does not mean that our anticipations are doomed to be disappointed. On the contrary, if life here has taught us anything through our experiences of our world, of work, of fellow-humans, of God, it is that illusions are the means of leading us to realities which eclipse them. As we look toward the unexplored beyond, we say to ourselves: "Eye hath not seen, nor ear heard, neither have entered into the heart of man the things which God hath prepared for them that love Him." We do not take the imagery of John on Patmos or of St. Paul as furnishing exact descriptions of the heavenly country. But experience taught them, as it teaches you and me, that the prime necessities for abundant life are usefulness, companionship, character; and it is these which they set at the centre of their visions: "His servants shall serve Him; and they shall see His face; and His name shall be in their foreheads"; "Now abideth faith, hope, love, these three." Suppose our hymns and prayers be largely symbols of our longings, this is not to say that when for us and ours death comes, these shall melt into thin air, and, like an insubstantial pageant faded, leave not a track behind. We are such stuff as dreams are made on. Our life from childhood, in work and friendship and love and religion, is of imagination all compact. Our experience leads us to expect that in death, as throughout life, for those who are journeying with God, the mirage shall become a pool. The New Jerusalem may be quite other than our social dreams imagine. But unless we pronounce fallacious all the testimony of generations, who marching through earth on the highway of holiness, have found the thirsty ground springs of water, the ransomed of the Lord shall come with singing unto Zion, and everlasting joy shall be upon their heads.

⇜§ THE WITNESS OF OUR HEARTS

Coleridge said of his youth: "My head was with Spinoza, but my heart was with Paul and John."

Most of us are more firmly gripped by men and women than by opinions. Count Tolstoi accounted for the first step in his change from pessimism to religious conviction by saying: "I saw around me people who, having this faith, derived from it an idea of life that gave them strength to live and strength to die in peace and joy." Lecky, surveying the growth of Christianity in the early centuries, wrote: "One great cause of its success was that it produced more heroic actions and formed more upright men than any other creed." And that remains true today. Face frankly the non-Christian interpretations of life—a godless, purposeless struggle, a race of dreaming and aspiring mortals bound to be engulfed in blank oblivion, an existence to be squeezed of all the pleasure it may yield ere its little day be over, and what sort of people take to them? One dare not speak slightingly of the intelligence or the honesty or the conscientiousness of many unbelievers; but are they the company with whom you would wish to trust the future of the community, or the future of your own children? If their views become dominant, what will happen to the idealism which they themselves hold over from a bygone faith? One may poke fun at the generation of the righteous. They often lack a sense of humor; they are sometimes wanting in taste; they frequently are not overstocked with brains—all serious deficiencies. But the amazing fact remains that despite these limitations, they sometimes turn the world upside down, and generally they do more than any others to keep it right side up. They may be guilty of glaring inconsistencies and of appalling stupidities; one can itemize a lengthy catalogue of the shortcomings of the saints, but without them there would not be the zeal, the dedication, the hopefulness, which initiate and carry forward earth's best enterprises. There come times when many of us are mentally bewildered, doubting the wisdom, or the goodness, or even the existence of God; but here is this company of believers who unquestionably stand for the type of life we prize, and to whom we recognize that our earth is indebted for the best it possesses. Can we betray them? Can we part company with them? Can we line up against them? A student at one of our colleges once phrased it: "I don't know where I'm at in my religion ideas; but I can't help seeing the bunch I ought to travel with."

◄§ RESURRECTION MADE REAL IN US

Many people still look at the question of immortality apart from the question of sin. They wonder whether they, as they are, or those whom they love, as they are, will survive death and be re-united. They are not concerned with the quality of that future life, nor with the kind of feelings and purposes which they or others can bring to it.

An acute observer of *The Human Situation* (as he entitles his book) has written:

> That mortals should desire immortality and
> yet find difficulty in passing an afternoon—if you
> have a fancy for paradoxes, here is a pretty one.
> We contemplate eternity without horror, and
> find an hour of our own society intolerable.

If one's existence seems made up of futilities, if one is frequently bored and has to use imagination "to kill time," what attraction is there in an everlasting boredom with the task of killing eternity? Worse yet, if life be a series of meannesses, ill tempers, impulsive blunders, calculated out-

wittings of others, which render them unhappy, which lower
social standards, and which add to the harshness of existence, what decent creature can wish to go on living to
poison with his presence any heaven into which he might
manage to slip? Thank God for a universe so firmly ordered
in righteousness that moral corpses are not admitted into
the enduring society of loyal hearts and true.

And thank Him more that the dead in sin can be raised
here and now by the grace of Christ to a life with Him in
which death is a mere incident. The right relations of
sin and death are made clear in our Lord's familiar words:

> I am the Resurrection and the Life: he that be-
> lieveth in Me, though he were dead, yet shall he
> live: and whosoever liveth and believeth in Me
> shall never die.

Christ first brings an inward Easter, and then sets before
us the Easter prospect of deathless life. Risen with Him,
who would not confidently and expectantly go on forever?

Nor is the victory, which is ours through Christ, this
inward conquest only. The resurrection was an event on
the broad scene of the world's history. The sinister forces
which opposed or ignored the Son of God were embodied
in institutions—in a mighty empire, in a venerable church,
in a capital city with its social habits and prejudices. These,
through a Pontius Pilate, through respected priests, through
a city mob, through the apathetic public, crucified Christ.
The world of that age, tragically duplicated in the world
of our time, resolved to get rid of One whom it found
troublesome, or just let Him be killed rather than be
bothered to protect Him. But He did not stay buried!
The course of things was reversed. The Roman Empire,
the Jewish Church, the city of Jerusalem, the world then
and ever since, has had Him to reckon with. That is the
indubitable fact of history. He is today man's most significant Contemporary.

✍ THE EXPECTANT CHRIST

Fenelon wrote the widow of a close friend of his:

> As for me who have been deprived of seeing
> him for so many years, I still talk to him, I still
> open my heart to him, I believe I meet him be-
> fore God; and though I do mourn him bitterly,
> I cannot think that I have lost him.

The only barrier between us and all who live with God is
the door which we keep closed to Him. Open that, and
many faces surround the central Face: "Ye are come unto
God, and to the spirits of just men made perfect, and unto
Jesus, the Mediator."

There are some who frankly dislike the thought empha-
sized by St. Paul when he writes of Jesus: "who is at the
right hand of God, *who also maketh intercession for us.*"
If God is our Father, why should another, however good,
intercede for us? The conception of someone using his
influence and putting in a word for us belongs to a political
past which we hope is outmoded. But this is to misunderstand intercession. When we pray for another, it is not an
attempt to alter God's mind towards him. In prayer we
add our wills to God's good will, our hearts to His outgoing love, our thought to His unfailing remembrance, that
in fellowship with Him He and we may minister to those
whom both He and we love. Trench has a sonnet which
expresses the satisfaction we find in giving our sympathy
through prayer:

> *When hearts are full of yearning tenderness*
> *For the loved absent, whom we cannot reach*
> *By deed or token, gesture or kind speech,*
> *The spirit's true affection to express;—*
> *When hearts are full of innermost distress,*

> *And we are doomed to stand inactive by,*
> *Watching the soul's or body's agony,*
> *Which human effort helps not to make less—*
> *Then like a cup capacious to contain*
> *The overflowings of the heart is prayer:*
> *The longing of the soul is satisfied,*
> *The keenest darts of anguish blunted are;*
> *And though we cannot cease to yearn or grieve,*
> *Yet we have learned in patience to abide.*

We are sharing with God all our desire for those dear to Him and us, and adding to His abilities to aid them as much as is in us. Can we imagine Jesus losing interest in those for whom He died, in the company who through the ages are carrying on His task? Can we imagine Him doing other than throwing His thought, His sympathy, His will, into God's mind and love and purpose for them? It must be a satisfaction to Him, the natural outgo of His affection and devotion, that He ever liveth to make intercession for us. The spiritual world is a realm of wills, and He is still saying to the Father: "Thy will be done," and flinging Himself with God into every purpose that means man's good, just as we fling ourselves into God's good will for mankind.

In the domed ceiling of an ancient baptistery in Ravenna, the figures of the apostles are portrayed in the mosaic in a circle at whose centre stands a throne, and it is empty. We cannot be sure what the fifth-century designer intended by that symbol. Was he thinking of the world of his day with its barbarities and wrongs, and trying to say that not yet had its rule been assumed by the Son of man? Or was he saying that those who in that baptistery took the name of Christ enlisted to make the throne of the world really His? Certainly it suggests something lacking and something which Christians must try to supply. He who is at the right hand of God stands expecting. We tell ourselves: "Behold, the Lord's hand is not shortened that it cannot save." We assure ourselves that ours, too, are "years of the right hand of the Most High." We know that the living Christ puts all the force of His mind and heart and will into the establishment of the reign of right-eousness. But the expectations of the Lord of heaven and earth and of His exalted Christ involve men and women of Christian conscience. The final scenes of our Gospels all express a confidence in those told to go, make disciples, feed My sheep, teach. Symbol of His sublime trust in you and me hangs that ascension portrait of One henceforth expecting.

◄§ OUR CONTINUANCE IN GOD

I suppose there are few of us who do not think now and again of associates and friends who have passed from us, and wonder what they would think and say of the current happenings of our day. And as we recall them, we often become aware how indebted to them we are for what they gave us. Whatever wisdom we possess for contemporary problems, above all whatever faith and courage and con-secration strengthen us to face the arduous undertakings which we confront, is not our own. It has come to us from God through them. At times we can almost feel the com-pulsion of their personalities upon ours. Their memories remain forceful inspirations. And further, if we think of them with Christ in God, they seem close to us today. Of the extent to which they know of the events of earth's dark history we cannot hazard a guess. We can be confident that, familiar with God's mind, they know all which it is wise and helpful for them to know. And we would not wish them to be earth-bound in their interests. Surely their present life is far too absorbing to have them continually looking backwards towards this shadowed planet where under God they had their education for the ampler tasks of the city of light. But whether ignorant or aware of what we face, their concerns and ours coincide. The will of God is their and our major interest, and that holds us firmly together. There are fine lines of Clough's in which he speaks of friends whom life has taken off into very different lines of service:

> *One port, methought, alike they sought,*
> *One purpose hold, where'er they fare.*

Such is the fellowship of Christians in God.

And because it is a fellowship in and with God it is a permanent fellowship. Once in the city of Edinburgh I was passing the Grange Cemetery, where there is a stone whose inscription commands attention. The stone was erected at the close of the first World War by a woman whose husband and three sons, her entire family, had given their lives in the cause of their country. She placed upon it their names, ranks and the places where they fell, and then an inscription of three words from a Psalm quoted in a New Testament writer: "But Thou remainest." All else gone, God was still hers. And with Him were those dear to her, and in Him they continued hers still, hers forever.

One might compare that stone with its satisfying inscription with the last lines from the pen of one of the profoundest writers of the last century—Emily Brontë. Tuberculosis had touched her with the hand of death, and she wrote:

> *No coward soul is mine,*
> *No trembler in the world's storm-troubled sphere;*
> *I see Heaven's glories shine,*
> *And faith shines equal, arming me from fear.*

And then, addressing God, she said:

> *Though earth and man were gone,*
> *And suns and universes ceased to be,*
> *And Thou wert left alone,*
> *Every existence would exist in Thee.*

"But Thou remainest"—that is all which a Christian needs to be sure of.

Our generation has little idea what lies just ahead. We are fairly certain that we shall find ourselves in a changed and unfamiliar world. None of us personally is aware what may confront him. If we put to ourselves or to those closest to us the Master's question: "Whither goest thou?" the immediate answer is far from clear. But it is the question which Christ wished His disciples to put to Him, that as He left them, with Gethsemane and Calvary in prospect, their minds might travel through and past them to His Father and their Father, to His God and their God.

✑ IN THE HEAVENLY PLACES

One of the saintliest Christians of the last century, F. D. Maurice, in an intimate letter to his wife, wrote:

> This day, twenty years ago, about the time I am writing, my sister Emma died. I believe she has been with me often, when I did not know it; and that we are really surrounded by all that we have lost. I do not think we bring them to us by our thoughts and recollections, but that they are present with us, and that we should believe it more, if we believed God was with us.

One dare not affirm that our Christian dead come to us. One would think and hope that their interest is not earth-centred, but directed to larger and loftier issues. Yet

Maurice is voicing a Christian conviction when he asserts that they and we are present to God, and therefore not completely sundered from one another, although our lives move in different realms. To the extent that we are occupied in God's purposes, we become alive to them. Both they and we are (to use a phrase of St. Paul's) "in heavenly places"; both they and we are together, as Christ put it, in our Father's many-mansioned house. If we carry the responsibilities laid on us up to God, and see our tasks, our burdens, our associations with men in His light, we are living beyond death's reach in things eternal.

But we do not lift ourselves to that level. It is the unique prerogative of Christ to open for us the door into this eternal life with God. Easter is the festival of the coming of the victorious Christ to those whose love makes His access to them possible, and of His raising them to His confidence and courage and hope in God. "When Thou hadst overcome the sharpness of death, Thou didst open the kingdom of heaven to all believers."

When Lincoln died, Stanton uttered the memorable saying: "Now he belongs to the ages." We can say no more of any figure in history. But the Christian Church says more of Jesus Christ. It is not only that He belongs to the ages, and that succeeding generations draw from His teaching and life and cross their highest wisdom and strongest stimulus to pursue it; but *that the ages belong to Him.* He is the living Master of each, its most significant Contemporary, in advance of its foremost ideals and dreams, and claiming its obedience and trust. To those who age after age accord Him their allegiance, He is alive in power. "They know whom they have believed, and are persuaded that He is able." It is this present ability to do for us and through us exceeding abundantly which attests to us that He is not among the dead, but the most Alive. He confronts us, claiming our loyalty and offering us His empowering comradeship—our life-giving Lord. And we men, whose love has tried to begin to do something for those given us, feel we must have them and go on doing for them forever. That very true friend, the poet William Cowper, wrote to Lady Heaketh: "You must know that I should not love you half so well, if I did not believe you would be my friend to eternity. There is not room enough for friendship to unfold itself in such a nook of life as this." Nor is there. Life is far too cramped to allow our sense of obligation for those given us to discharge its duty and unfold its love. And life is quite roomy enough to have both them and us grow to mean so infinitely much to each other that without them we do not wish a second life. Our Christian outlook touches with everlastingness the ties which link us and those whom God has given us. "Father, I will that they also whom Thou hast given me be with me where I am." If Christ so prayed, after the same manner pray ye and be confident of an answer.

And it was a prayer that He, Himself, took pains to guarantee. "While I was with them, I kept them in Thy name." And such keeping anchors men forever. You may recall how Matthew Arnold voiced the feelings not only of Thomas Arnold's own children but of scores of Rugby boys when he wrote of that great schoolmaster:

> *But thou would'st not alone*
> *Be saved, my father! alone*
> *Conquer and come to thy goal,*
> *Leaving the rest in the wild,*
> *We were weary, and we*
> *Fearful, and we in our march*
> *Fain to drop down and to die,*
> *Still thou turnedst, and still*
> *Beckonedst the trembler, and still*
> *Gavest the weary thy hand.*

89

> *If, in the paths of the world,*
> *Stones might have wounded thy feet,*
> *Toil or dejection have tried*
> *Thy spirit, of that we saw*
> *Nothing—to us thou wast still*
> *Cheerful, and helpful, and firm!*
> *Therefore to thee it was given*
> *Many to save with thyself;*
> *And at the end of thy day,*
> *O faithful shepherd, to come,*
> *Bringing thy sheep in thy hand.*

Lo I, and those whom thou hast given me.

❧ THE MOUNTAINS OF GOD

Have you ever set out in a canoe, early in the morning, for a hike up among the great mountains, when the whole landscape was shrouded in mist, and felt yourself moving in a strange and almost weird world, aware of vast but concealed presences? Then, as the sun rose above the hilltops, and the mist started to run up the mountainsides, familiar outlines began to show themselves, and, at last, there were the mountains of God in all their grandeur. May not the awaking Yonder be somewhat like that? We shall find ourselves moving perplexedly, conscious of vastness all about, but as we grow wonted to our novel surroundings, will they not be the well-known everlasting hills of God—the heights and glories of the friendly life of His heart and conscience? We shall recognize the familiar principles of truth and beauty and righteousness we have glimpsed here. Whatever may be the forms of its expression, we shall see life, orderly and adaptable and lovely, everywhere upsurging and the spirit's life of faith, hope and love, dominating and crowning all other life. "The throne of God and of the Lamb shall be therein."

PRAYERS

O God, who in the resurrection of Jesus Christ hast assured us that love cannot be defeated by selfishness and hate, nor knowledge vanquished by ignorance, nor life holden of death, put new heart and hope and determination into us and all followers of Jesus to proclaim and stand for His Kingdom, in faith that all power in heaven and earth is confederate with him who obeys the Son of man.

Enable us to bring to the empty grave all our own purposes of good that have miscarried, our best hopes as yet unrealised, our struggles for righteousness still unsuccessful, the disappointments which have made us doubt Thy love, and to confirm in Christ's triumph our confidence that however long the crucifixion may last, however securely buried may seem our aims of good, our plans of love, our trust and hope, the stone shall surely roll away, and all that is truly right and loving and Christlike prevail, through Him whom Thou hast made the Lord of life forever.

O Father, who didst exalt to Thy right hand Thy Son, our Saviour, Jesus Christ, and hast made the name of servant which He bore to be above every name, and the love He showed in life and death higher than aught else in the esteem of men, join us so firmly to Him in obedience and trust that He may even now lift us to dwell with Him in the heavenly places, that while on earth we may share the thoughts and sympathies and purposes which are His on high.

Let the triumph of His resurrection and ascension minister comfort to all who suffer and are sad. As a cloud once received Him out of men's sight, assure us that behind every obscuring cloud lies the heaven where love comes to its rightful place. Bid the lonely and mourning see in Him the forerunner who has prepared a place for His people, and receives them unto Himself, that where He is, there they may be also. And this we ask in Jesus' name.

Eternal God, before whom stand the living and the dead, we praise Thy name for ten thousand times ten thousand in the world unseen, whose faith lives on in our souls, whose knowledge lights our path, whose tasks have fallen to our hands, and especially for friends whose faces we see no more but whose love is with us alway. Grant that as we hold them in grateful remembrance the sanctity of their goodness may hallow our earthly days and devote us to diligent labor and trustful patience, until Thou bring us with them to the company of the saints in light, through Jesus Christ, their Lord and ours.

Father of our spirits, from whom we come and unto whom we go, and from whose love in Christ Jesus our Lord neither death nor life nor things present nor things to come nor height nor depth can separate us, Thou art our dwellingplace in all generations. We thank Thee for all who have faithfully lived and peacefully died, for all enriching memories and uplifting hopes, for the sacred and tender ties that bind us to the unseen world, for the dear and holy dead who encompass us like a cloud of witnesses and make the distant heaven the home of our hearts. Make us followers of those who through faith and patience now inherit the promises through Jesus Christ our Lord.

Our Sins, and Our Saviour

The Bible suggests three sources of temptation. Two of them speak of an intruder from without who instigated a man to sin, just as today we sometimes phrase our question: "What got into him? what possessed him?" In the early narrative of David's reign, written in an age when God was believed active in every event, He is said to have stirred David's vanity to number his fighting men. "The Lord moved David, 'Go number Israel and Judah.'" Some centuries later an historian, re-telling the incident, finds it impossible to charge God with inciting David's pride, and ascribes the temptation to a sinister subordinate who goes about making trouble in the Almighty's world. "Satan stood up and provoked David to number Israel." Then several centuries later still, a New Testament writer discards the idea of an outside *agent provocateur*. God tempts no man; Satan is not mentioned. "Every man is tempted, when he is drawn away of his own lust and enticed."

The last explanation has appealed to modern men. Sir Walter Scott makes his discerning heroine Jeanie Deans tell Madge Wildfire: "There's nae devil sae deceitfu' as our ain wandering thoughts." George Meredith concludes a sonnet:

> *In tragic life, God wot*
> *No villain need be! Passions spin the plot.*
> *We are betray'd by what is false within.*

Control the demon inside yourself, and you need fear nothing else in earth or heaven. That is rugged individualism; and it is bracing doctrine breeding responsible men.

None of us likes to admit guilt for wrongdoing. We are adept at passing on the blame. We explain that we were unfortunate in our parents. They were too strict, or too lax, too aloof, or too affectionate; and they "conditioned" us. Or we were born at a trying epoch—the hey-day of American capitalistic expansion, when it was inevitable that we should be contaminated with self-indulgent materialism; or we were reared in the war years which left their fell mark on us, confusing our moral standards or unleashing our passions or brutalizing our natures.

Current psychology adds to these moral alibis. Men and women have themselves analysed, and find emancipation in banishing the ugly names which vigorous religion attached to sins when these are re-christened with labels with no suggestion of guilt. They are maladjusted, or introverted, rather than dishonest or selfish. A middle-aged father tires of his wife and becomes involved with a young woman half his age, and is told by a practitioner that he is suffering from "a spasm of re-adolescence," when he ought to be struck in the face with "Thou shalt not commit adultery."

And the present pre-occupation with social conditions seems also to furnish excuses. A student who does not concentrate on his work, and has a discreditable record, solaces himself with his concern over the international situation, and may even plume himself that he could not be absorbed in studies when war clouds darken the horizon, and fascism or communism lifts its menace over many lands. Any of us who has let himself get into debt, or made a mess of his family relations, or allowed affairs entrusted to him to become at sixes and sevens, is likely to ask: "What can one do in a time like this?" It does not occur to us that almost every age in human history has been confused, that the skyline has seldom been without threatening storms, and that men and women have tried resolutely to shoulder their loads, and perhaps carry some of the burdens of others, and have sought (in the language of the New Testament) to live "unspotted from the world."

ક્ક WHEN CHRIST TAKES POSSESSION

It is because Christ can go beyond the threshold of our
thinking and penetrate into the innermost recesses where
emotions rise, that He can save us. We sometimes talk about
decisions for Christ, as though we made up our minds and
gave a reasoned verdict. In fact, you and I are Christians
not because we choose to be; we cannot help ourselves. It
is not a matter of decision, but of compulsion. Christ has
made His way, by doors we know little of, into the very
fabric of our being. By coercions from within, coercions
that arise from deeper sources than we can explore, He
constrains us.

Indeed, most of us know that we are Christians in spite
of ourselves. As we survey our record, it is a tale of forget-
fulness, indifference, blundering, betrayal. We seem to
have done almost every stupid and foolish and mean and
faithless thing to thwart the Spirit of Christ. The weak,
blind, perverse flesh has been with us unfailingly. If there
is any good in us, it is not our own. If we have been of the
slightest use to man or to God, the credit is not ours.
We were apprehended, and then again and again arrested,
and kept hold of, by Christ Jesus. We have no self-assur-
ance. Who dares underwrite his own fidelity? Think of
our chronic lapses, our repeated failures, our continuing
deficiencies, our trying and provoking and irritating characteristics, but He has not given us up. "If we are faithless,
He abideth faithful." As deep, as persisting, as tenacious
as our mortal flesh is this strange Figure, who entered our
human world centuries ago, has kept on in it ever since,
and has managed to get into you and me, and to hold on to
us with an unshakable grip. Yes, deeper than our will
which decides, far deeper than our mind which explains

why, down at the source of our feelings is this potent Presence, Jesus alive within our mortal flesh.

This is our ultimate ground for hope. Human nature in many of its doings and misdoings makes us shudder. To suppose that it is unalterable would fill us with despair. But in the Man, Christ Jesus, it was taken possession of. The word became flesh and we beheld His glory. And all down the corridors of history are lights which He has illumined. In these courageous and believing souls He has made His presence manifest. The malignant forces in mortal flesh barbarously working disaster in our time and threatening yet blacker catastrophe summon us and all Christians to a bolder hazarding of ourselves for Jesus' sake. And if human nature is terrifying in its devastating powers and pitiable in its blindness and helplessness, by God's grace it can also become in those who venture with Him the disclosure of that divine life which is the light and hope of the world.

ᴥᴥ IF WE WANT TO BE BETTER

Jesus does incalculably much for us of which we are not conscious. His coming is like the sunrise. We have no idea what the sunlight does for our bodily health, our brightness of spirit, the vitality of all living things. Occasionally on a sparkling day we stop and exclaim what glorious weather! But for the most part the sun's blessings are taken unrecognized. There is no way of computing how much worse off our world would be had Jesus not come. All of us, whether we acknowledge any indebtedness to Him or not, are vastly different because of factors He brought into our race's life.

But no man gets His best from Jesus unconsciously. The richest gifts are for those who look at Him in wonder and tell Him what they wish He would do for them. "What wilt thou that I should do unto thee?"

Here is some hampering peculiarity—some twist or bent —which we have allowed to warp us, and make us difficult for those who work at our side, or which prevents us from meaning very much to our families, or which gets in our own way and inhibits our usefulness. We may label our impeding propensity by some new-fangled name, drawn from the vocabulary of current psychology. It is this or that complex or mechanism or anti-social mode of behavior. Or we may recognize it more clearly under some old-fashioned name. It is pride or jealousy or lust or acquisitiveness or cowardice or laziness or suspicion or plain vile selfishness; indeed, it usually can be labelled that in the end when we unmask its various disguises. We may tell ourselves that we were conditioned in this way by our parents or our upbringing or our schooling or by the circumstances under which we have had to work. We may be honest and own up that our own giving in to ourselves has allowed something which once was a minor weakness to become a major malady, interfering shockingly with what we might be and do. And here it is—our unfortunate propensity—that about us which compels those who characterize us, after they have said everything commendatory they can think of, to add "but" and then to detail this limiting and nullifying factor. It is possible that we may not realize what our besetting difficulty is; we may be self-deceived. But most of us have revealing moments when we can see that we are nuisances to good folk who wish to work with us, and that we are hindered from signifying much to those we love best, and that something spoils our work or prevents us from doing anything that really helps.

"Thou shalt call His name JESUS, for He shall save His people from their sins." The wonderful fact is that He can take these twists and biases of ours, and actually get rid of them. But it cannot be an altogether unconscious process. "What *wilt* thou that I should do unto thee?" We have to look plainly at our limitation—our prejudice, or envy, or timidity, or self-centredness, or temper, or feelings— and then tell Him that we will to be released from it. Jesus put the question to another: "Wouldest thou be made whole?" It can be done. He has done it with ten thousand times ten thousand.

❧ THE SIN-BEARERS

The world is pushed forward by men who care; but it is lifted to companionship with the heart of God by men who share. It is easier far to denounce failures and insist on betterment than to own that we are implicated in the failure, that the weakness or badness of other folk may be traceable to some extent to kindred frailties and iniqui- ties in ourselves, and that in any case no sin of theirs is without a near relative in our own defects. You recall Christina Rossetti's denunciation of another:

> *Clearly his own fault. Yet, I think,*
> *My fault in part, who did not pray*
> *But lagged and would not lead the way.*

Sin-bearing fathers and mothers, sharing as they well may the deficiencies of their children, sin-bearing citizens accepting responsibility for national selfishness and the collective injustice of society, sin-bearing churchmen acknowledging our obligation for the pettiness, the apathy, the want of imagination and daring and passion in the world-wide company who bear Christ's name, sin-bearing friends who feel as their own the weaknesses and twists and self-centredness of those who live with them—these are they who raise men to be comrades of the Father who is afflicted in all His people's affliction and shamed in all their sin. They know the fellowship of Christ's suffering; but the pain is incidental. Primarily they know the fellowship of Christ's conscience. And the conscience of Jesus is the conscience, the essential goodness, of God.

PRAYERS *Mon. noon*

O God, our refuge and strength, to whom we never turn in vain, grant us Thy succor in all the circumstances and experiences of life. When our faith wavers and the vision of Thy face grows dim and the things we see appear far more real than the unseen; when we are tempted to grow cynical, to think contemptuously of people and to do mean things; when we are called to difficult duty or lonely responsibility; when we are weary of work that seems barren of result, and irritated with shallow or flippant or selfish people; when the unknown future fills us with misgiving and we forget Thy changeless love and care, be Thou our help, O Father, whose mercies never fail.

Tue. noon

O Thou who causest the sun to shine upon the evil and upon the good, and art Thyself more radiant in Thy love than the noonday brightness, lift upon us the light of Thy countenance, that in Thy light we may see light—light upon every hidden fault and secret meanness, light upon every doubt and fear, light upon every interest and duty, light upon every cross and care. Shine upon our ignorance as the light of truth, upon our perplexity as the light of faith, upon our sin as the light of purity, upon our sadness as the light of comfort, upon our broken ties of affection as the light of immortal life.

And beyond the shadows of our earthly scene, where we

guess and grope our way and often err, we look with thanksgiving to the land that stretcheth afar where eyes behold the King in His beauty, and to that city for which the Lamb slain is the everlasting light; and with the innumerable company of its citizens, among whom are those most dear to us, we confess our faith and offer our prayer in words they used in the days of their pilgrimage, saying with one heart and voice: Our Father who art in heaven—

Wed. noon

Gracious Father, whose mercy is higher than the heavens, wider than our wanderings and more enduring than our obstinate sinning, receive back to Thyself Thy perverse and tiresome children. Thou seest through our disguises and pretenses. We cherish Thy Word, but do not follow its counsels; we bear Thy Son's name, but are not ruled by His mind; we claim brotherhood with Thy children, but are sundered from them by prejudice and self-interest. We feel the confusion and wrong of our world, where millions suffer needless poverty, where nations and races dwell in mutual fear, where justice is flouted by greed and wisdom scorned by stupidity, and we fail to acknowledge the world's sin our own. Cause us to look in and see there all we condemn in others. Cause us to look up, and see thy grace to us. Move us to repentance and to a life worthier Christ our Lord.

We commend unto Thee those dear to us from whom we are separated; We also bless Thy name for our beloved who have been withdrawn from our sight, but are with us always in Thee. Teach us to live in the strength of the heritage they have bequeathed us and in the power of that endless life which we share with them through Christ, the Saviour and Lord of us all.

The Comradeship
of the Living Christ

The early Christians never give the impression of looking back and following a pattern laid down either in the words or the example of Jesus. They acted spontaneously from their own consciences made sensitive by their fellowship with Christ. Freedom is one of their outstanding characteristics. They are not obeying a rule, or reproducing a model of the past. The mind of Christ in them governs their thought and stimulates it to work out solutions to the questions of their time.

Readers of Walter Pater's *Marius the Epicurean* may remember the occasion when Marius witnesses the gladiatorial games at Rome held under the eye of that noble stoic philosopher, the Emperor Marcus Aurelius. "Weary and indignant, feeling isolated in that great slaughterhouse," he is angry that Aurelius can be so impassive to horrible suffering. Pater comments:

> What was needed was the heart that would make it impossible to witness all this; and the future would be with the forces that could beget a heart like that.

It was this heart which Christianity created.

Suppose one of Marius' Christian friends had put a manuscript of the Gospels into the hands of the Emperor, and told him that here he would find the answer to all the moral questions in the government of his empire, how baffled the Emperor would have been at these collections of conversations, and incidents, and the accounts of the execution and startling return to His own of a strange Figure of the past century. Here is no specific guidance for a statesman; indeed most of his problems were never envisaged by the Galilean. No! but the Figure in those writings was concerned to make over the Emperor, and enlist him with a new spirit to reconstruct his empire.

Jesus is not a giver of rules, but a maker of men. He fought legalism in the religion of His day. It is ironical that the Church recurrently tries to make Him the sponsor of a fixed pattern of action. The final scene on the Gospel pages, represents Him leaving His followers not a law or a set of precedents, but breathing on them His Spirit and committing to them His mission.

In Pater's book Marius had a Christian friend, Cornelius, with a quality which intrigued him:

> Some inward standard Marius seemed to detect there (though wholly unable to estimate its nature) of distinction, selection, refusal, amid the various elements of the fervid and corrupt life across which they were moving together:—some secret constraining motive, ever on the alert at eye and ear, which carried him through Rome as under a charm.

Jesus possesses the mysterious power to weave Himself into the fabric of the conscience of those who respond to Him. Instinctively they judge everything by its Christlikeness or un-Christlikeness. He sits regnant at the centre of their beings. That is His authority over us. It is not a position to which we have consciously elected Him. We seem to ourselves to have had little choice about it. Through His words, His life, His cross, His impress on men, He takes hold of us, sways our judgments and moulds our convictions. We do not so much assign this place of lordship to Him as recognize that He has taken and occupies it. We cannot get away from Him. Emerson once said: "His name is not so much written, as ploughed into the history of this world." He has made Himself a permanent factor in the moral background of our race. There He is. We can

turn our backs on Him, and go counter to Him; we frequently do. Still He haunts us. Whenever we think of Him,
He is better than our best. This gives Him His grip on us.

✍ AS GOD IS KNOWN IN JESUS

The experience of finding God through Jesus has repeated itself again and again. Do you recall the story of
Raskolnikov in Dostoevski's *Crime and Punishment?* A
heady student in St. Petersburg University, full of the
rebel theories of the flaming youth of his epoch, he asserts:

> I am the final judge of my own thoughts and
> deeds. . . . Who dares to tell me what I am al-
> lowed and not allowed to do?

He goes the length of murdering two unfortunate women
with whom he had become involved. He justifies himself
heartlessly:

> Am I not free to kill a loathesome, disgusting
> woman, if I find it convenient to do so?

He is apparently without compunctions or regrets. Then he
meets a young girl, Sonia, whose step-mother has compelled
her to walk the streets a prostitute to earn money for the
family, but who has remained a singularly pure and devout
soul. She and Raskolnikov are pictured in a bare low-
pitched room, lit by a single candle, when his eye falls on
a Bible, which had been given to Sonia, and he asks her to
read. She opens at the eleventh chapter of St. John. "Her
voice" writes the novelist, "rang out like a bell, triumph and
joy gave it power." Through that story of the raising of
Lazarus, from the lips of this abused but lovingly devoted
creature, Christ, the Resurrection and the Life, spoke to
this murderer, moving him to repentance, so that he gave

himself up to justice, was banished to the penal colonies of Siberia, but went a new man.

It is through the grace of Christ, often re-embodied in frail but believing human beings, like this girl, whom fellow-convicts call "our dear good little mother," that the love of God lays hold of men transformingly. They are not theorizing about God, but witnessing to what He means to them when they start with the grace of Jesus Christ and go on to the love of God.

Let me put beside the Russian novelist's character an incident which occurred in New York City a generation ago. There was a brilliant Jewish schoolteacher in one of the higher institutions, who had been reared in orthodox circles, and as a student had left them to join the Ethical Culture Society, at that time under the inspiring leadership of Dr. Felix Adler. In a single winter she lost by death the man to whom she was engaged and her mother, and in her bleak loneliness the Ethical Culture Society seemed chill and comfortless. Through a Christian fellow-teacher she started attending a church, and after some months she came one day, under great emotion, to speak with its ministers. She said: "I see it now."

"What do you see?" he asked.

"I see that all I adore as divine is there in Jesus; and all I need a God for He does for me."

This again was not theory: this was discovery. Through the grace of Jesus Christ God makes His love known and felt.

And who is God? We may mean by that one syllabled word of three letters the vast inscrutable Mind and Force behind and in this Universe with all—pleasant, tragic, comic—that goes on in it. How bewildering life is! How poignantly men ask: "What can its Creator be like?"

No observer of the world and its intricacy can question the vastness of whoever or whatever is back of it. An eighteenth-century poet describes David the psalmist:

> *He sang of God—the mighty source*
> *Of all things—the stupendous force*
>   *On which all strength depends;*
> *From whose right arm, beneath whose eyes,*
> *All period, power and enterprise*
>   *Commences, reigns and ends.*

A century later, when further scientific thought had made the universe even more wonderful and complex, the novelist Thackeray, protesting against those who think they can exactly define the Almighty, exclaims:

> O awful, awful Name of God! Light unbearable! Mystery unfathomable! Vastness immeasurable! Who are these who come to explain the mystery, and gaze unblinking into the depths of light, and measure the immeasurable vastness to a hair?

We dare not forget of whom we speak when we say "God."

Nor must we take from His greatness. Our generation in particular needs a vision of One limitless in wisdom, in resource, in power, to meet the overwhelming situations of our day in human history. You may recall words ascribed to Sir Francis Drake, when the great armada was approaching the shore of Britain:

> Never was fleet so strong as this, but the Lord of Strength is stronger.

This huge and intricate scheme of things, from bulkiest planet to tiniest insect, attests His greatness.

But what is *He* like? It is frightening to fancy limitless resources in the hands of a cruel despot or an uncaring waster. And when we survey the pageant of human history from the dawn man to the miscellaneous mortals, saints and devils and the numerous intervening mixed characters, who are our contemporaries, how ambiguous appears its hidden Controller! It is only when the gracious Figure of Bethlehem, Galilee, Gethsemane, Calvary, lays hold of men, that we hear them declaring "God is love."

☙ THE COMMANDING ATTRACTION OF CHRIST

Jesus prevents smug contentment—and that is something. But with most of us He does more than that. He constrains us to abandon some things we enjoy. He compels us to shoulder responsibilities we should like to dodge. He forces us to undertakings from which we shrink. And He keeps us at them when we should much prefer to be released.

On a college campus a student who had flung off the restraints of his home and school training and was headed for moral disaster, when reasoned with to stop, said bluntly: "I feel that I ought, but I don't want to." And for a while he didn't. Subsequently, he managed to get himself in hand and to redeem his college standing. And when asked what had happened, he remarked: "I just had to quit: something out of my Christian training rose up and grabbed me." He was unconsciously repeating the apostle's metaphor: "I was *apprehended* of Christ Jesus."

And not only as a check on moral self-destruction is Christ potent. Men tired and disheartened in their battle with social forces find Him a commander with authority to hold them to their warfare. When the Jesuit scholar, Father George Tyrrell, was attempting to induce the Roman Church to face the results of scientific and historical investigation and to accord her scholars freedom, and found himself pitted against a crushing ecclesiastical tyranny, he wrote in a letter:

> Again and again I have been tempted to give
> up the struggle, but always the figure of that

strange Man hanging on the cross sends me back
to my work again.

Jesus still possesses authority.

And He has power to make us in the fight to which He
conscripts us more than conquerors. The student whom I
cited was enabled to pull himself up abruptly. Tyrrell lost
his battle, and was excommunicated, but his books had and
have a wide reading, his spirit is still a force to be reckoned
with, and he went down with colors gallantly flying. The
quality of soul of which Jesus is the supreme symbol is
unconquerable. The conscience He embodies is the mightiest force of which we know. Let any combination of factors
range themselves against that, and sooner or later they are
broken. What can you name more compelling than the
Spirit of Jesus? He can do with us and He can make us do
more than any other power in the universe. That is His
authority.

✑§ LEARNING BY OBEDIENCE

Jesus would probably not waste much time over our confusions. He might take them for granted. He Himself knew
what it was to be baffled and puzzled: "O My Father, *if* it be
possible"; "My God, My God, why?" But He would certainly
ask us whether His touch had not made anything visible.
"Seest thou aught?" And the most perplexed here finds that
Christ's contact with him makes something clear. One says:
"I see that human nature is much more capacious than is
commonly thought. A plain man can be what that Carpenter
of Nazareth was, so I believe in and hope for much from
myself and from my fellow-humans." Another: "I see the
force of love, like His. Explain Him as you may, there is
no denying the fascination of His cross, and the grip such

devotion gives Him on masses of people. Even when I am disposed to scrap His beliefs as first-century notions, His self-sacrifice seems to me timeless. It gets hold of me, and puts me to shame when I live by lower motives." A third: "I see the abiding power of His ideals. Centuries have rolled by, and His hopes have often been called impossible dreams; but despite men's failures to take Him seriously, here are His visions of brotherhood still haunting mankind. We cannot get away from them." A fourth: "I see the charm of His religious faith. I do not know whether there be a fatherly God such as He trusted or not, but I see how desirable that God would be, how He would fit in with and complete and make reasonable and possible the best hopes of the best men." A fifth: "I see that when I actually try His faith, when I act as though He were correct, when I pray, when I assume that in Christlike attempts I shall be divinely reinforced, I am not disappointed. I cannot explain it; I feel myself dealing with that which is mysterious, but I am upborne, fortified, energized." A sixth: "I see that those who sincerely give themselves to their Master always seem satisfied. I do not hear them saying, 'I have followed Him, and there is nothing to it.' On the contrary, they get what they think they want to such an extent that they become enthusiastic, and wish everybody else to enjoy the same allegiance. And for myself, I am frank to say that I see that every regrettable occurrence in my own career has come from disregard of Him, and the few circumstances that content me most in retrospect are those in which I tried to be governed by His Spirit."

Need we go on with this enumeration? Let the most unbelieving, the most mentally confused, who has ever had a sense of Christ's touch on him, ask himself what he sees in consequence of that touch, and there is not one who does not see something, and something marvellously worth seeing.

What then? Why not stay with Christ and get a further touch? If the contacts we have had with Him through home influences, through education, through friends, through reading, through the Church, have not done everything for us, if today we look out on life with imperfect vision, it is not to the point to complain of the imperfection, but to remind ourselves of the vision. Christ has always made men see what apart from Him they would never have noticed. As a matter of history He has made our race see in man, in God, in life, in death, in every experience, what had not been seen before. It is quite true that they have usually seen dimly. The partially cured blind man told of in the Gospel of Mark might have run off exulting that he saw men at all, and contented himself with his blurred eyesight. That is what multitudes of Christians have done, and are still doing. Christ's hands laid on them through some contact gave them glimpses, surprising glimpses, and they have rushed off to live and act and think by them. They have seen, they surely do see, something. Many of them are not sufficiently thoughtful to recognise the blur in their vision. When they try to tell others what they see, the blur is there, and others looking with their vision see men as trees walking. Hazy views of God, of duty, of forgiveness, of sin and its consequences, of the application of the Spirit of Christ to this or that phase of life—this is all that the Christian Gospel means to a great many—a bank of fog pierced by occasional shafts of brightness. Well, seeing through a haze is far better than total blindness. The most imperfect seer sees something. And if Christ's hands at one touch bring this much of vision, why not remain for a second touch? The only danger is in the man who leaves Christ. At first he may be so delighted that he sees anything that he runs off to live by his half-sight. Then he may be so disgusted that he does not see clearly that he drops into living as though the light of Christ were not light at all. His wisdom lies in remaining with his Enlightener and letting Him again and again and again touch him to clearer seeing.

ᴈᴈ NOT SERVANTS, BUT FRIENDS

Through myriad hints, man has come to find himself in a haunted universe. Things about him and within him have inferences. He cannot get away from the feeling of Something or Someone unseen to whom they point. More sensitive spirits have dimly discerned what and who this mysterious Soul of the universe is. Some have been very sure of God, and in that faith have been able to achieve singular triumphs. One in particular has seemed to be His intimate—to understand Him more clearly, to share His purpose more fully, to be more congenial with Him than any other. No one else dared say "Come unto me, all ye—." And what Jesus was and remains casts a spell over us. We cannot say that we understand God, that we know what He is doing with us and ours, that we know His ways in this baffling world. But Jesus we know. This Man of Nazareth and Calvary draws us to Him with an irresistible friendliness. He will not call us servants, but friends, and He wishes us to share all His secrets. We cannot; but that is not His fault. We are spiritually too immature. But He draws us into His companionship, and we find ourselves in our childish way entering into His faith, and saying "Our Father," becoming comrades of His purpose and seeking to bring about the reign of that Father's love in our earth, entering into His hope that such love shall rule both here and in all the mansions of the Father's eternal home, catching Jesus' Spirit and trying to think and act with His mind. Through Him we feel ourselves linked with a vaster world than we can understand, connected with purposes that sweep in orbits far beyond our thought, made partners in momentous business where the relatively small things which we do from day to day have eternal significance.

↫ THE EVERLASTING APPEAL OF THE CROSS

Shortly after the return of Colonel House from the deliberations which issued in the Versailles Treaty, I happened to be present at a small luncheon with him. In the course of the conversation on events in Paris, he remarked: "In the midst of our discussions, the thought occurred several times: 'If only we could stop and reflect what would Christ think of this or that proposal, our discussion would have been raised to a higher level, where solutions might have been easier to reach and far wiser.'"

Colonel House did not mean that Christ could give specific guidance on the political and economic questions which he and his colleagues were discussing. Such problems have to be met with the best political and economic wisdom at hand. But above and beyond human thinking is Christ Himself. To lift Him up in thought is to let light from His cross shine on our plans to judge and to purify them. And in facing Him men are drawn to Him and to each other in Him so that a fellowship of spirits is knit.

There is something altogether fascinating in the Crucified to which men of all sorts instinctively respond. In April 1848, three young Englishmen, all subsequently distinguished, found themselves on a holiday trip in Paris in the midst of the revolution which overthrew King Louis Philippe. The men were Jowett, a future Master of Balliol, Stanley, later Dean of Westminster, and Palgrave, a poet and later the editor of the *Golden Treasury*. Palgrave kept a diary of their trip, in which there is an entry describing the sack of the Palace of the Tuileries by the mob. Everything was being smashed, when suddenly the mob reached the chapel, broke in the doors, and found themselves confronting the huge painting of Christ crucified behind the altar. Someone called out: "Hats off." Heads were bared; most of the crowd knelt down; and the picture was carried out to a neighboring church in "the most utter silence—'you might have heard a fly buzz.'"

That Figure, lifted up in men's minds and hearts by His exalting influences throughout the centuries, exerts its pull on their deepest feelings. We, in this judgment day on our world, must, with our contemporaries, think with every bit of brains we have, in order to settle wisely the bewildering issues which face us. Our wisest intelligence seems pathetically insufficient to achieve enduring harmony. Thank God for the gift of His Son. We must keep Him uppermost in our thought, and lift Him up before our neighbors, fellow-countrymen, allies, enemies. He will draw us and them unto Himself. And in Him "all hold together."

✒ WHEN WE ARE LED BY GOD

Think of the occasional revealing day when it suddenly dawned on us to what we were being *led.*

Think of things denied us on which we had set our hearts, things for which we wept at the time. That was a handling of us with bit and bridle: very likely we bless God for it now.

Think of the responsibilities that came to us without our seeking, of the friends who just walked our way, of the happinesses that took us by surprise, of the strange comforts that softened our sorrows. Is it an exaggeration to say that the best things that have enriched us have been unexpected gifts for which we did nothing and which we certainly did not deserve?

Think of the push given us every now and again, and the

steady pressure which has forced us to our most useful work. John Muir, the naturalist, put it tellingly: "I feel as if a Divine Hand has been laid on my shoulder." Goethe said: "*Must* is hard, but it is only when a man *must* that his real inner nature is revealed. Anyone can follow his own caprices." Sometimes the "must" was bit and bridle—the compulsion of circumstance—sometimes it was the guiding Eye, the coercion of conscience: "I can do no other."

Think of the follies and the meannesses and the conceit and the sheer selfishness of which we have been guilty, and of the faithfulness of Him who still endured us and disciplined us. "I was as a beast before Thee," says one of the psalmists, and the Hebrew word which he uses is "behemoth," the creature scholars say in the Book of Job is a hippopotamus. 'I was a clumsy, thick-skinned, stupid, hoggish creature before Thee. Nevertheless I am continually with Thee." God did not get disgusted with us. He did not deal with us as brutes. He did not kick us out of His path. As a man his son, "Thou hast holden my right hand."

And if there are some matters in His dealings with us which are still altogether unintelligible, if we cannot answer some of the whys which our hearts ask—why this was laid on us? why that was taken? why this was permitted?—we are not astonished that the complexities of life should puzzle us and the wisdom of God transcend our minds. Few of us, so far as our own lives go, are disposed to question the line of the hymn:

> *With mercy and with judgment*
> *My web of time He wove.*

A. C. Benson wrote of a close friend of his:

> He had to bear a series of devastating calamities. He had loved the warmth and nearness of his home circle more deeply than most men, and the whole of it was swept away; he had depended

for both stimulus and occupation upon his artistic work, and the power was taken from him at the moment of his highest achievement. His loss of fortune is not to be reckoned among his calamities, because it was no calamity to him. He ended by finding a richer treasure than any that he had set out to obtain; and I remember that he said to me once, not long before his end, that whatever others might feel about their lives, he could not for a moment doubt that his own had been an education of a deliberate and loving kind, and that the day when he realized this, when he saw that there was not a single incident in his life that had not a deep and an intentional value for him, was one of the happiest days of his whole existence.

It is the insider's view alone that is intelligent. "Thou shalt remember all the way which the Lord thy God hath led thee."

Life as it comes to us is baffling. We are living in a generation which seems to be witnessing the passing of much that is familiar (called bad or good) and the coming of—well who knows just what? We may disagree as to what is going and what arriving, but we all agree on the perplexity of the immediate present. Are we to muddle our way through with only such wisdom as we pick up from fellow-mortals or carry in our own heads at the risk of blocking God's purposes and having to be pushed aside or got round? Are we to be whipped along, the hacks of circumstances which get on our backs and ride us? Or are we resolving to be companionable with the Most Wise and alert to His eye?

A Scottish divine on an errand in this country not long ago stopped off at Niagara, and wrote this description of his visit to the Cave of the Winds:

It is like living amidst the break-up of an old universe or the creation of a new. You are shut off from the whole world of nature and humanity for the time, enwrapt in this wild smother of thunder and foam. Your only link with the entire world of humanity is the pressure of the hand of your guide. You cannot see him, you cannot hear him; all that you are conscious of is a hand with a pull in it.

This tumultuous world of ours rolls and roars about us. Explain it how you will, Jesus takes hold of us and pulls. He is the link with the divinest we can imagine—our truest symbol of the Hand of God. To let Him grasp us, committing ourselves utterly to Him, and to live responsive to His pull—that for a Christian is to be led by our wise Father in His eternal purpose.

PRAYERS

O God, by whose tender mercy the dayspring from on high visited our earth and many centuries now have known in Jesus the light of life, cause us to set ourselves to our several tasks as children of His day. May the clear shining of His love search our souls, quickening every holy aspiration and every passion for justice, and withering all selfishness and distrust. And grant that by the faithful labor of thy Church in every land and the loyal lives of all who bear the Christian name, He, the Sun of righteousness, may illumine the whole earth, that the hurts and bitternesses of many generations may find healing in His rays, and that the races and nations of men, dwelling together in His brightness, may reflect in their work and play, their thought and speech, Thy glory once manifest in the face of Him, our Lord and Saviour, Jesus Christ.

O God, who dost beset us behind and before, we bless Thee for kindnesses which look forth upon us from our yesterdays, for hopes which beckon from our morrows, and for Thy presence today. Thou comest to us in the affection of our homes, in the loyalty of friends, in questions which wake our minds and needs which claim our service, in the wisdom of books and teachers, in the heritage of saints, and lo, Thou standest in the midst of our thoughts in the house of prayer. They of old time tell us that Thou art a guiding cloud and fire to them who seek justice and freedom, a stern corrector of the selfish and faithless, a home where the believing of every generation are at one. And we have found Thee all and more than has been told us—a rock beneath our unstable feet, a high tower in the day of battle, a brook by the way of which we drink and lift up the head, a mount of vision whence we see the path of duty and the land of heart's desire. Thanks be unto Thee for all Thou hast been and art to us, O God.

*The Enlargement of Life
in God*

There is a depressing view of human history which keeps telling us that nothing much is accomplished in a single lifetime. But is that true? Was nothing permanent achieved when Abram went out from Ur, or when Moses led his people through the Red Sea, or when the prophets set before Israel and mankind the righteousness of God? Was nothing eternally significant completed when the Son of God bore men's sins in His own body on the tree? There have been days of the Lord whose effects continue transformingly through thousands of years. Why should we think that we, who have mysteriously been set down in a crucial generation, cannot in our lifetime, yes in this very year, by what we under God and with His grace think, do and bear, bring to pass results in the relations of nations and races and of men one to another which shall render earth divinely better for whatever further ages it may pursue its course? One day with the Lord a thousand years!

The naturalist William Beebe tells of visits he made to Theodore Roosevelt, another naturalist. After an evening's talk in Roosevelt's home at Sagamore Hill, the two men would go out on the lawn and gaze up at the sky and see who first could detect the faint spot of light-mist beyond the lower left-hand corner of the Great Square of Pegasus, and then one or the other would recite:

> *That is the Spiral Galaxy in Andromeda.*
> *It is as large as our Milky Way.*
> *It is one of a hundred million galaxies.*
> *It is 750,000 light-years away.*
> *It consists of one hundred billion suns, each*
> *larger than our sun.*

After an interval Beebe reports Mr. Roosevelt would grin at him and say: "Now, I think we are small enough. Let's go to bed."

It requires that perspective of God's eternal purposes to keep us conceited mortals in our place as little children.

When we are in the depths of discouragement because things in which our hearts and consciences are bound up are faring badly, there is no tonic comparable to this: "A thousand years" are with the Lord "as one day." It is a message which has meaning only as we are sure that the cause to which we attach ourselves accords with the Lord.

And if our human plans for a great purpose are sincere efforts, we can have faith in *them*, too. When the founders of this nation were striving to get the self-seeking thirteen independent colonies, each jealous of its own interests and rights, to adopt the constitution, New York was among the most difficult to persuade. The Convention met up the Hudson at Poughkeepsie. After long debate, when the voting began, ratification was defeated again and again 46 to 19. Alexander Hamilton, the protagonist for the Constitution, kept on fighting. A friend asked him one day what the prospects were. He replied:

> God only knows. Several votes have been taken by which it appears that there are two to one against us.

Then he added:

> Tell them that the Convention shall not rise until the Constitution is adopted.

THE FINAL DRIVING POWER

In his fascinating biography of the Adams family through four generations, James Truslow Adams notes in the third generation "something lacking that had constituted a driving power hitherto." John Quincy Adams, confronting the premonitory storms over slavery in Congress, and foreseeing the terrific struggle ahead of the nation, "did not for an instant lose his faith in God and the fundamental morality of the universe." His son, the war-time minister to Britain, had the New England conscience of his ancestors, but without their firm belief in the Puritan God. His son, Henry, in turn, writes of his own early days: "The children reached manhood without knowing religion." The driving power, so characteristic of the family up till then, vanished.

The grace of God, as believing men have discovered, is not just a genial goodwill towards His creation. It is not God's good-naturedness. It is God giving Himself energetically to make out of those who let Him creators like Himself. Luther put it:

> God's grace is something strong, mighty and busy; it is not something that lies inert in our souls as those dream-preachers pretend. . . . Nay, it carries, it leads, it drives, it travels, it does everything in a man.

Yes, it was that which Paul had discovered. The gracious God does all that when a man gives him the chance to. "His grace which was bestowed on me was not in vain, but I labored more abundantly."

◢§ IN OUR MIDDLE YEARS

It usually takes the experience of at least middle life to appreciate the graciousness of God. By that time we have had our disillusionments. Few of us have been as useful as we hoped to be. The air-castles of our confident expectation prove clay-hovels when we find ourselves in them. We are apt to grow cynical. Most men and women need a rebirth in their forties.

One of the conservation problems of recent times has been the use of old newspapers. Could not some process be devised by which they could be remade, and our forests spared to that extent? The most serious difficulty chemists encountered was to get rid of the printer's ink. But at length a method of de-inking them has been discovered, and they can again be reduced to pulp and remade into clean paper. Life imprints upon our minds a mass of stuff—some of it bitter, some of it false, some of it obscene, much of it trivial. By middle age most of us want to be de-inked and start afresh. Well, it can't be done altogether, of course; it probably should not be done. But the fact is that when God makes His face shine upon us, many things imprinted on us by circumstances and people and our own inner strivings fade out. So is the Lord gracious unto us.

Again, most of us need a re-warming to our work in the middle years. The first enthusiasms have died; we are more open-eyed to the difficulties, less confident of coping with them. Honest folk have been brought to a fairly low appraisal of themselves. Lord Charnwood, writing of Abraham Lincoln at the age of forty-five, says: "Middle-aged and from his own point of view a failure, he was set upon making himself a bigger man." That resolve was surely God's grace to him and to our country.

A reading of biographies is discouraging in that it so often appears that the creative period in men's careers came early and was brief. So many of the best things in poetry, in music, in art, come from the relatively young. Hazlitt wrote of the middle-aged Coleridge: "All that he had done of moment, he had done twenty years ago: since then, he may be said to have lived on the sound of his own voice." Like the sunlight in spring, bringing again the lovely life of May, religion re-creates. It is a middle-aged Moses who led his people out of Egypt, and a middle-aged Paul who pens his greatest letters and does his outstanding missionary work. The freshness of our earlier powers may be gone, but when God makes His face shine on us, there is a rebirth and release of vigor.

> *But let me only think of Thee,*
> *And then new heart springs up in me.*

The most serious peril of the middle years—"the destruction that wasteth at noonday"—is conventionality. In youth we are rebels against things as they are; but rebellion proves a hazardous and fatiguing enterprise, and before we know it, we are accepting situations and fitting our ideals with considerable whittling to the grooves and holes already cut. It is then that God's face shining forth on us throws the landscape again into its distinctions of shade and brightness. Bad is bad and good, good; and with a second morning of vitality we go out to do battle. And it is not just the rebellion of protesting youth over again, but a maturer, more clear-seeing, more patient and more resourceful warfare. We fight not for ourselves only, but for our younger companions. A Paul draws his sword for Timothy and Titus and Mark and Luke. His veteran presence steadies and emboldens them. That's God's graciousness to the middle-aged.

✑§ USING LIMITATIONS

The Book of Job portrays a resolute soul trying to push past the hedge of tradition and of his own ignorance and obtain a more intelligent view of life and of God. And Job succeeded. Ever since his day those who have entered into his spiritual heritage have lived in a roomier place for souls. Some of our limitations are due to man's stupidity and injustice; others to our own laziness and folly. Brave men of courage and persistence have broken through them. Heartening chapters in history have been written by those whose faith moved mountains that hedged them and their fellow-mortals in narrow and dark valleys, and by those whose determination and industry increased their own knowledge and powers to serve God and man. We are never to call our limitations God's hedge, until we are sure that neither we nor others can remove them.

But there is still a hedge about Job to the end of his story, and the main word of God in the book about it recalls its two sides. It shuts us *off* and it shuts us *in*.

It shuts us *off* from temptations. We seldom ask of our restricting hedges: From what do these protect me?

Here are our limited abilities. How we chafe that we cannot do a lot of things that we should like to do, nor do far more cleverly what lies within our power! Even Shakespeare speaks of himself in a Sonnet,

> *Desiring this man's art and that man's scope.*

But how perilous more art and more scope might have been to his work! Dr. Samuel Johnson once said roundly: "Sir, a man may be so much of everything, that he is nothing of anything." Versatility may be the Satan from which we are safely hedged. We lack this, that or the other art or skill. We do not possess the scope of others in the one or two arts and skills which are ours. Thank God for defending us from the temptation to dissipate our energies and waste our time. When once we realise that the other side of our hedge is the Satan of diffusion, like Wordsworth,

> *We learn to live*
> *In reconcilement with our stinted powers.*

Here are circumstances that tie us down to just one task—financial necessities, obligations for others, limited health, the exacting demands of the task itself—and every now and again we grow rebellious. We consider ourselves hedged in to a contracting routine. Yes, but what of the Satan on the other side of that imprisoning hedge? What would we get done without that daily grind? What service would we render unless we were circumscribed in that routine? Some men have had to build their own hedges in order to accomplish their tasks. Victor Hugo sent his clothing out of the house when he was writing *Notre Dame* lest he be tempted to go out before he had finished it. Napoleon Bonaparte declared: "Il faut se limiter," and it would have been far better for him and for Europe had he set his hedge about a much narrower plot. If God in His providence has built the hedge about us, remember the Satan outside, and be thankful for its protection.

But of more importance is it to ask of the hedge: To what does it shut me in?

Job, in this drama of a soul, cut off from his herds, deprived of sons and daughters, doomed to illness, exposed to harassing friends who insisted on repeating traditional notions obviously inadequate to interpret his case, faced with his own insufficient thoughts of God, is forced to think and think and think, and finally to stop thinking and contemplate the wonder and mystery of the world, and listen to God until he reached a fellowship that passed his understanding:

> *Now mine eye seeth Thee,*
> *Wherefore I abhor myself, and repent*
> *In dust and ashes.*

The Scottish minister and poet, George Matheson, was blind. After serving for a number of years in a quiet parish in a town on the banks of the Clyde, he was called to a difficult charge in one of the shabby, crowded, low-lying districts of Edinburgh. I recall in student days making my way on a Sunday morning down into this unattractive neighborhood along dreary streets, entering a cheerless barn of a church, with a congregation of working folk, and then seeing this outstanding poet-preacher led up into the pulpit. When Dr. Matheson laid down his task, he said:

> I came a taper amid the torches (the lights in the Edinburgh pulpits). My place was down in the valley—the Stockbridge Valley. . . . There you will see man outside the stage with the lights suppressed and the music silent, and the dancing ceased—man unconventional, man natural, man struggling hand to hand with life's poverty and toil. These were the masses before which I stood —an atom in the crowd. It was a tragic spectacle; it was blind Samson with his hands upon the gates of Gaza. The Philistines laughed; but I think I lifted these gates one inch. And I think that next to the strength of God, and next again to your kind cooperation, I was indebted to my own weakness. These sons of toil said, "Here is a man with an environment no less unfavorable than ours— barred by every gate of fortune, yet refusing to give in—overtaken by the night, yet confident of the morning. . . ." My sermons may have flown over your heads like the bird of Paradise; but my life has been level with your own—an obstructed life, a circumscribed life, but a life of boundless sanguineness.

There was a servant of God asking, To what am I hedged in? and acknowledging his imprisoning blindness to be God's assistance to his ministry.

✺ THE ONE THING NEEDFUL

In dealing with any situation, how necessary it is to know what to brush aside as of no consequence. The Marthas attempt to include everything and all seems equally important. The Marys with the emphasis of Christ say: "This is big; that doesn't matter. This advances the cause; that, however desirable, we can get on without." Bishop Burnet said of King Charles the First: "He minded little things too much, and was more concerned in drawing a paper than in fighting a battle." Like the hapless Charles, you and I are in the thick of a fight, a life and death struggle for the throne of the world. Can we make Christ master of our business life, or is the clash of interests to end in a violent and unspeakably destructive revolution? Can we render His Spirit Lord over a commonwealth of free nations, or are we to witness another and far more awful earth-wide war? Can we place Him in control of this and that man or woman or little child, now aimless, or ugly-tempered, or habit-gripped, or hard as nails? Can we let Him have His way with ourselves, or must we go on making a mess of our lives, and letting them mess the lives about us? "One thing is needful" —all else relatively trifling.

Even in getting on with God, how indispensable to know what to omit, what not to be troubled by! Canon Ainger once wrote to a friend: "In religious knowledge, as in all other things, dare to be ignorant of many things, that you may have time and brain and heart for a few things." Of how much in God's way with men and with Himself Jesus dared to be ignorant! Why were there lame and halt and lepers in Israel?—the mystery of suffering; why were there some men with five talents, some with two, and some with one?—the mystery of inequalities; why were some born blind, physically and spiritually, and some who did not possess ears to hear?—the mystery of handicaps; why was this and that assigned to Him?—the mystery of personal experiences. Only once do we overhear Him asking Why, and even He went unanswered. But daring to remain ignorant, with nothing to say about dozens of questions concerning God, which men have raised since time began, He was engrossed in His Father's interests, and He had time and brain and heart to receive and body forth more of God than all the rest of the universe together contains.

It amazingly simplifies life when One who knows puts His finger on just one thing and tells us "That is the essential." A second-century Christian uses the very phrase we have employed when he writes to his correspondent, Diognetus, concerning Christianity, and calls it "This new interest which has entered into life." It is, says Christ, "the one thing," and it is "needful." Do we possess it?

Interests are caught by contagion. One man cares intensely, and others become infected. Here is the purpose for which Jesus thought, toiled, poured out His blood, and ever liveth—the world of men linked in friendship with the living God. Does it interest you and me? Does it interest us supremely?

SERENITY IN OLD AGE

Old people are often depressed. They may be lonely, for so many comrades are gone. Their physical vitality is low. They feel themselves set aside. They grow sad and talk of "the good old times," and are puzzled by the strangeness of the present day. The peace which they need is a renewal of confidence and of courage. It is the fashion to disparage the Victorians. One wonders whether this generation will match the high-hearted old men of the last century. To mention statesmen only, think of Palmerston becoming prime-minister at seventy, of Disraeli leading his party at seventy-five, of Gladstone introducing the Home Rule Bill at seventy-seven and relinquishing office at five and eighty. There was something vitalizing in the spiritual atmosphere of that disesteemed age.

And it is pre-eminently the function of religion to keep believers vigorously alive. You may have read Saint Beuve's complaint of the paganism of Montaigne, who, he said, had

> no notion of that inverse moral and spiritual perfection, that growing maturity of the inner being under the withering of the outer envelope, that perpetual education for heaven, that second birth and immortal youth which makes the white-haired old man seem at times only in his first bloom for the eternal springtime.

In a very beautiful letter, Jowett, the Master of Balliol, insists:

> Though I am growing old, I maintain that the best part is yet to come—the time when one may see things more dispassionately and know oneself and others more truly, and perhaps be able to do more, and in religion rest centered in a very few simple truths. I do not want to ignore the other side, that one will not be able to see so well, or walk so far, or read so much. But there may be more peace within, more communion with God, more real light instead of distraction about many things, better relations with others, fewer mistakes.

That is not complacency, but serenity. It comes to those who are mellowing in the light from an unseen world. The task for all of us, as years advance, is to ripen—ripen in wisdom, in sympathy, in fairness, in patience, in love. So many men instead of ripening, rot in spots and harden in spots. Instead of harmony there is peevishness, instead of self-command, fretfulness. It comes from absence of the eternal sunshine. Life has lost its everlasting relationship. We cannot ripen ourselves; we ripen in the light and warmth of Another. You and I are sojourners in the earth as were all our fathers. But the devout are sojourners before God, passing like the rest of men, but passing into a brightening day. "The Pilgrim they laid in a large upper chamber, whose window opened towards the sun-rising; the name of the chamber was Peace."

PRAYERS

O most holy and loving God, we thank Thee for the quiet rest of the night that has gone by, for the promise that has come with this fresh morning and for the hope of this day now before us. While we have slept the distraught world in which we live has swept on, but Thy faithfulness has not ceased to care for Thy children nor do Thy compassions fail. May we now trust Thee this day for all the needs of body, soul and spirit, and with unwavering mind seek Thy kingdom and Thy righteousness, through Jesus Christ our Lord.

Almighty and ever-living God, who art beyond the grasp of our highest thought but within the reach of our frailest trust, come to us in the beauty of the morning's light, in the tasks of this day, and reveal Thyself to us. Enrich us out of the heritage of seers and scholars and saints into whose faith and labors we have entered, and quicken us to new insights into Thy mind for our time, that we may be possessors of the truth of many yesterdays, partakers of Thy thought for today, and creators with Thee of a better tomorrow, through Jesus Christ, the Lord of the ages.

O God, unto whom Thy saints of old offered a morning sacrifice, with this new day we bring Thee our minds and strength that our every thought may be informed by Thy wisdom and our every power employed for Thy will. We present before Thee our families and friends, that the ties which bind us to them may link them and us to Thee, our Father in heaven, and be purged of selfishness and ennobled by Thy love. We offer our devotion to our country, that our patriotism may be freed from prejudice and envy, and made as broad as Thy goodwill towards mankind. Accept us as we take up our tasks; purify our inmost selves and the outward selves we share with those who shall meet us this day; and use us beyond aught we ask or think for Thy purpose in Jesus Christ our Lord.

*Christian Marriage
and the Christian Family*

If individuals are bundles of inconsistencies, it is not surprising that marriages are difficult unions and that families fall apart. For man and wife—each an assortment of incongruous qualities—to fit into each other and think and work their lifelong in unison—that is a miracle. For parents and children, brothers and sisters, and the annexed in-laws who are added to a family circle—all to form a harmonious group—that, too, is a miracle. There are the worlds of the different generations, the worlds of diverse interests, the worlds of varying tastes and capacities, to be held together.

Now Christ has by no means always seemed to unify families. Nor does genuine personal devoutness invariably make people easy to live with. John Wesley's wife was unquestionably a very trying woman, but listen to a letter which that flaming evangelist and tireless servant of Christ wrote to her:

> Suspect me no more, asperse me no more, provoke me no more; do not any longer contend for mastery, for power, for money, for praise; be content to be a private, insignificant person, known and loved by God and me. Of what importance is your character to mankind? If you were buried just now, or if you had never lived, what loss would it be to the cause of God?

A present-day American wife receiving such a letter would board the first aeroplane for Reno, and that letter would suffice as evidence for extreme "mental cruelty." John Wesley was a consecrated man, but that letter does not suggest the thirteenth chapter of First Corinthians.

The fact is that we are such mixtures that we cannot help being trying even to those who most devotedly love us. We can never take for granted that it is easy for them to put up with us. Marrying "in the Lord" (to use St. Paul's phrase) not only involves marriage based on agreement in loyalty to Christ. That is much. Two Christians will patiently try to hold together with the love which beareth all things. But if marriage is to continue a Christian partnership, and if a family is to possess a Christian home, husband and wife, parents and children, must take their thoughts of and for one another, their home ways, and scrutinize them in the light of Christ. Our highest affections may be inconsiderately possessive; our devotion be mixed with impositions on others' love. Remembering what inconsistent creatures we are, we become tolerable only by submitting and resubmitting ourselves to Christ's control, and by His grace we may be honorable and lovable to those who share life with us. "In Him all things consist."

✑ WHEN RELIGION IS LACKING

There is nothing more pathetic than to see a household where hearts are in sympathy at all other points but one, and that one devotion to Jesus. For husband and wife to be able to share everything but that which to one of them is the supreme thing, faith; for parents and children to be in complete accord about everything but that one thing which must either be all-in-all or not at all, is the saddest of home tragedies. Are our home circles one in Jesus Christ? Do we kneel not merely each himself at his own bedside in private prayer, but all together in family prayer? Do we sit together while one reads from the word of God, or perhaps each with Bible in hand and reading a verse in turn, one in our desire to hear the voice of our one Master and obey it? Is our family one in the house of God, or are children sent while father and mother stay away, or do parents have to come without their boys and girls because Christ has not the interest for them He has for father or mother? "In Him all things hold together," and until every life in a family circle has been tied fast to Jesus the home is not firmly, strongly, lastingly complete.

THE COST OF THOUGHTLESSNESS

It is a soul-satisfying feast that is spread when life is wedded to life in friendship and in love. What a banquet is set before us in sympathy and comradeship and devotion! And these are supremely the things for which God Himself cares, so that in enjoying them to the full we are most completely at one with Him. But here, too, the thoughtless man excludes himself. A few ended friendships are broken by a bitter quarrel or some sordid treachery; but most terminate because the friends slip out of one another's minds. How often one wakens remorsefully to say: "I wish I had thought"! It is the things we forgot to notice and which it did not occur to us to do which stifle friendship; for its vital breath is attention. Some marriages are shipwrecked by a sudden disloyalty; but vastly more are started towards disaster because husband or wife does not think enough, and so unwittingly wounds or injures the other. Here Hood's line is most certainly true that "evil is done for want of thought, as well as for want of heart." The gravest peril in both friendship and wedded love is that they make us selfish. We presume upon them. We take the lavish devotion given us as a matter of course. We lack imagination to see what the King often expects of those who come to the royal feast. It does not occur to us, any more than it did to the dull fellow in Christ's parable of the wedding feast, that there is no place for us at the banquet of the heart without an appropriate garment. "A man that hath friends must show himself friendly." He who would enjoy love in its fulness must remain a lifelong lover. Woe to us if we do not realise that friendship and love are the holy feasts of the great King. We dare not stumble into them unthinkingly. A peremptory voice will some day demand of us: "Friend, how camest thou in hither, not having a wedding garment?"

WHERE IS THE RIGHT AUTHORITY?

There is a vexatious question that may arise in many homes. We have had epochs of restraint by parental authority, and that may still seem effective up to a point; then the growing boy or girl revolts, and the years of repression are likely to be succeeded by years of rebellion; and the home becomes wretchedly unhappy for both parents and children. Or more recently it has been common to see the opposite course tried, where children are allowed to be unrestrained, to develop their individualities unfettered, and to do exactly as they please. The result appears in boys and girls, and later grown men and women, who are the slaves of their own emotions or caprices, and are pathetically handicapped for life—unfit for marriage, or for teamwork in industry or politics or the church. We do not cultivate a field by allowing it to express itself, for we know that its self-expression will be a crop of weeds, which have seeded themselves. Unsown and uncultivated human nature does not express itself any more satisfactorily. It receives the prolific suggestions of the life round about, and becomes waste land full of the common moral weeds of the community.

Occasionally one discovers a home where parents are ruled by a vision. It may be a broad vision of the progress of mankind, and embrace many engrossing interests—the whole world's life become the Kingdom of God; or it may be a much narrower vision of some particular public interest. But whether inclusive or restricted, if they dedicate themselves to it unreservedly, and share it with their children, it becomes the accepted purpose of the home. Boys and girls from their earliest days feel that life has a supreme meaning. They know that father and mother do not put their own comfort or convenience first; that they have no selfish ambition for their children. They know that they keep themselves in training for one end, and cordially accept the limitations this puts upon them. It is the topic of which they talk at table, of which they read, and read to their children, for which they pray, and pray with their children. Unconsciously, the children are laid hold of by the vision which masters their parents. It becomes natural for them to shape their plans to fit in with the family purpose. As they grow up, the vision will probably assume a somewhat different form for them than it has taken for their parents, but they cannot think of themselves as other than socially obligated lives, committed men and women. Their own inclinations and moods will not lead them lawlessly; vision has formed conscience. They will not throw off responsibilities and grow restive under social restrictions. The vision of the community—its needs, its possibilities, its claims on them—possesses them. They are self-disciplined for the sake of that to which their vision commits them.

And this is true of the relation of husband and wife. "Where there is no vision the people cast off restraint." Partnership for life with even the most congenial companion involves give and take; and as the years pass man and wife may develop along different lines, and become much less congenial to each other, so that they grate upon each other and seem to stifle each other's aspirations. If they make an effort and hang on to an unhappy married life through sheer will power, there may come a day of fatigue, when they will give up, and let the home crash. If they have vision, vision of the homes of the community and the damage to the family ideal of one more domestic tragedy, vision of their children's lives pitifully disordered by sundered parents, they accept the restraints which life together imposes upon them both. And in the end they will find themselves not suppressed and distorted, but ennobled and enlarged. Vision has led them to lose themselves for the sake of the community, and in so losing themselves, they find themselves.

◦§ REDISCOVERING OUR FATHERS' FAITH

Any normal child accepts eagerly the God whom the family and the community sincerely believe in. His vivid imagination to which the unseen is as actual and often more actual than the seen, his trustfulness, his desire for companionship and dislike of being left alone—all equip him to believe firmly. Many children think a great deal about God, take Him into their practical considerations, and treat Him as a very present member of the household and neighborhood. Those who deny their susceptible minds this religious satisfaction do them a cruel wrong and vastly impoverish their early years. Older folk whose own faith is not frankly expressed, who cannot bring themselves to speak naturally of God and do not lead children to talk to Him in family prayer and in public worship, fail to provide boys and girls with that vital religion in which they can gladly and outspokenly live as children of God.

But in most cases, even where both home and community have been sanely and sincerely believing, maturing young people pass into views of the world and outlooks on life from which the God of their childhood is omitted or in which He appears passing strange. These young folk are not necessarily less earnest or less conscientious. As a rule, they are more thoughtful, more idealistic, more socially minded and better informed than many of their elders. They can usually teach us a great deal which we need to learn. But for the time being they may impress us as quite godless, and they may declare themselves without faith.

Fortunately, this is rarely the final stage. Ancestral voices reawaken and speak persuasively. Robert Louis Stevenson, writing of some clergyman among his forbears, said: "Try as I please, I cannot join myself on with the reverend doctor; and all the while, no doubt, and even as I write the phrase, he moves in my blood, and whispers words to me, and sits efficient in the very knot and centre of my being." Life's ordeals and strains throw us back on whatever reinforcements are available, and few sober-minded folk go through middle age without re-examining the religion of their forefathers, and without discovering, underneath superficial coverings which they may be disposed to discard, solid and substantial convictions on which they can rest, and stand firm. When they ask themselves what they shall hand on to the next generation, it is usually to no great extent that which they and their contemporaries have improvised, although each age has some genuine gains to add to the racial inheritance, but far more important in their eyes is the stalwart trust, the imperious conscience, the believing courage of truly godly ancestors.

✒ USING THE BEST WE KNOW

In any situation in this world we find the stock of instruments at hand for our use limited. The temptation is often to give up the work or withdraw from the battle, saying, "What use is there in my trying to do anything with this clumsy implement?" Or else to pick it up despondently expecting to find it very awkward and good for little. We have to learn that the sword available under any circumstances in a world over which our God rules must be the very best sword for us, and to grasp it heartily, with words like those of David when he saw the sword of Goliath, "there is none like that; give it me."

Here, for example, are parents faced with the problem of training their children to be good Christians. They feel that they know next to nothing about the Bible. They didn't pay very close attention when they went to Bible School themselves. They haven't kept up the habit of reading the Bible carefully every day. They hesitate to try to teach their children for fear that they may ask questions they cannot possibly answer. They would like to have family prayer, but the father has never prayed before anyone before, and he shrinks from letting his family hear him stumble through some faltering sentences. So because they are so poorly equipped they attempt nothing.

Suppose they were to sit down and select a simple Bible story and try to get what appeals to them out of it for the benefit of their children, the very fact that they have to be so simple with themselves will probably make the story more interesting to their children. The few plain sentences the father can utter with halting speech and faltering voice will impress his family more with his sincerity and earnestness in trying so hard than if he could patter off glibly a lot of phrases. Take all that's available, whatever of the Bible you know, whatever gift of prayer you possess, confident that God has put at least that much in your hand for His work. What God gives is never inadequate. "There is none like that, give it me."

PRAYERS

thur. noon

Most gracious Father, from whom every family in heaven and on earth is named, bestow upon these Thy children the seal of Thine approval and Thy blessing, enabling them faithfully to perform and keep the vow and covenant betwixt them made. Render them alway worthy of each other's unfailing reverence and steadfast love. In their companionship may every joy be doubled and every sorrow eased of half its bitterness. Bind them in one Spirit as helpers of each other's faith, bearers of each other's burdens and comrades of each other's purposes of good. By their union increase their usefulness to the Kingdom of Christ, assisting them to dedicate their united lives to Him, and empowering them more and more to serve Him with all that is theirs. Except Thou, O Lord, build the house they labor in vain that build it; and we beseech Thee to inspire every plan they cherish for their home, and to grant them continually wisdom, courage and patience to fashion it after the mind of Christ. Fulfill unto them the desires of their hearts exceeding abundantly above all that they ask or think; and be Thou, O God of their fathers, their joy, their portion and their home forever, through Jesus Christ, the Lord of life and love.

Fri. noon

O God our Father, we pray for our homes, that loyal love may hold fast husbands and wives, that boys and girls may grow up reverent, courteous, and public-spirited, and that from our generation and the next Thou mayest find many quick to see and eager to respond to every call to service and sacrifice, that Thy cause may not lack leaders and whole-hearted followers, and that in our day Thy kingdom may advance with power.

We pray for all who are worn by illness, all who are ill-used or forgotten, the lonely, the disillusioned, the victims of their own folly or of the harshness of others, little children given false ideals and deprived of the inspiration of Jesus, youths and maidens launched on life's voyage without chart or pilot, men and women staggering under their loads and strangers to the Burden-Bearer, those amid the shadows of evening without expectation of the dawn of a fairer day. Pitiful Saviour, grant them Thy salvation.

And we thank Thee for Thy servants of all the ages whose warfare is accomplished and who have won home to Thine eternal light and peace, and we pray that Thy good gifts of faith and courage, of gaiety and a tranquil heart, may be upon us, that we may be meet to dwell with them in Thy presence, through Him who is the Author and Finisher of faith, Jesus Christ, thy Son, our Lord.

Sat. noon

O Father, to whom we are all little children, we commend to Thee this day the boys and girls of our congregation, praying that in home and school and the Church of God they may be led to prize truth, to revere justice and to think of themselves as servants of men, above all that early they may be brought to honor and cherish Thy holy Child, Jesus, and to walk with Him as their Friend and Master all their days. Dedicate afresh parents, teachers and pastors to their training and fill us with wisdom, tact, patience and enthusiasm for their sakes. And grant that children may be used to lead us to a childlike heart towards Thee, that we may be reborn to their confidingness, their curiosity to discover new knowledge, their zest for life, their unconquerable hopefulness that tomorrow has in store that which is better than any yesterday; through the leading of the Holy Spirit.

❧ Inspiration
    for Everyday Duties

In one of Scott's novels David Gellatley describes Bailie MacWheeble as "a particularly good man, who has a very quiet and peaceful conscience, that never did him any harm." But most of us have consciences that take us in hand and badger us and bother us and force us to this, that and the other duty. When one has enjoyed the relaxation of a vacation, how disagreeably domineering are the insistent voices of our tasks or of the claims of others on time and patience and energy! One might cordially accept the calls of one's regular and expected work, but how resentfully one listens to the interrupting voices which break in on one's schedule and insist on being heard and will find an ally in our own conscience that asserts: "Listen, you know you ought!" Well, how shall we label this inward voice that conspires with all manner of people and situations and events and keeps forever strapping burdens on our backs and facing our minds with problems and goading us on to outlays of energy and pointing us to additional tasks? Many men do not stop to give it a name, but they respond to it reluctantly as to a slave-driver. They grimly set their teeth and resolve to do their duty. And all praise to them for their conscientiousness, however joylessly they go about the thing which is laid on them. There is a hardness about conscience that makes even a Christian call its voice "stern." You remember Wordsworth's famous Ode which begins:

> *Stern Daughter of the Voice of God!*
> *O Duty!*

But the instant his mind has linked that voice with God, the God and Father of Jesus Christ, sternness cannot be the whole description:

> *Stern Lawgiver! yet thou dost wear*
> *The Godhead's most benignant grace;*
> *Nor know we anything so fair*
> *As is the smile upon thy face:*
> *Flowers laugh before thee on their beds*
> *And fragrance in thy footing treads.*

How are we labelling the intrusive calls that day after day press themselves upon us? Are they "My obligations, my load, my problems, my family or business or civic responsibilities?", or "my Father's assignments to me, the extras with which my Father is interrupting what seemed the whole program He had laid out for me, when I faced it this morning"? Don't you see the amazing difference it makes whether we connect these things with God or not, and with the God whose name we know in Jesus? If these duties are just mine, and laid upon me by circumstances or my inherited moral sense or the accepted ethical standards of the day, then I have merely myself and the good-will of equally conscientious people to rely on. If they are my Father's and mine, and my Father is the Lord of heaven and earth, then what measureless resources I can draw on and be sure of receiving! "Our sufficiency is of God."

What's in a name? "In the name of the Lord will we set up our banners."

৺ AHEAD OF THE CROWD

Religion always separates us from the common life of men. From childhood it gives us a feeling of detachment: we do not belong to the mass of mankind—we belong apart. We are not to conform to the ways of the world; we have other standards. We are forced to draw the line at this and that which society considers quite correct. Boys and girls of our age do thus and so; but so do not we because of the fear of God. We have loyalties to a Church, to a Bible, to a Sunday, to Christian principles, which we discover many people think odd and perhaps ridiculous. One might imagine that this sense of separateness was the worst kind of preparation for a comradely character. It often does make young people a bit rigid and possibly priggish. But it is a necessary element in forming characters that are helpful to men's deepest needs. The detachment from the common life is essential if we are to be attached to God. That higher attachment lifts us above ordinary standards, supplies more inclusive and tenderer sympathies, sends us back with finer consciences, and makes us aware of fellowship with One who is Father and Friend of all. Religion isolates that it may consecrate. It unties us from the bundle of human life and fastens us to the heart of God in order that with that bigger and warmer comradeliness it may tie us again more closely and to far more people than we felt bound to before. This is the process by which good men are produced.

✍§ LIFE'S REQUIRED COURSES

The curriculum of our life and death is mostly made up of required courses. There are occasional electives, but even they surprise us by leading on to other courses that have to be taken. Jesus' characteristic word is not "I will" but "I must." If the inevitable is not forced upon us by circumstances outside our control, we are driven to it by our own consciences. It is the pressure from without and the coercion from within that makes us effective:

> *Ah, the key of our life, that passes all wards,*
> *opens all locks,*

> *Is not I will, but I must, I must, I must, and*
> *I do it.*

But be sure we *do it*. God's will is never merely to be endured; it must be shared. When we say, "Thy will" to the God and Father of Jesus Christ, we are not thinking of a blind force that pushes its resistless way through time and space, and to which puny man can only submit. "Thy will" is for a purpose with such love in it as has flowed these centuries from that cross at Calvary. In every inevitable a Father's hand stretches out to us. We rise and take it. The inevitable is here, delightful or dreadful, but we face it together. "I must," we say, "and with Thee, my Father, I do it."

◦§ DRESSED-UP TEMPTATIONS

Temptations never appear terrible. If they did, they would cease to tempt. Many hard things have been said about the devil, but no one has ever alleged that he did not know his business. Dr. Johnson in his essay on Milton remarks: "There is little in Satan's speeches that can give pain to a pious ear." That proves that Milton knew something of the hero of his poem. Temptations come urbanely and suavely, and give us no jolt or jar to put us on our guard. They come, like the Gibeonites, assuring us: "We are your servants." All undesirable allies, who would entangle us in compromising leagues, know how to approach us most civilly. "In vain is the net spread in the sight of any bird."

But every decision in a world like ours is a much more perilous matter than we fancy. Browning's Pope at eighty-six assures us:

> *All to the very end is trial in life.*

And it is not the big ordeals—the Jordans to be crossed and the Jerichos to be captured—which are the most hazardous. Every Canaan has its wily Gibeonites. They are lurking for us in some apparently casual remark at a dinner-table to commit us to assent to an opinion at variance with the mind of Christ. They are hiding in a letter that lies on an office desk to inveigle us in a proposition which does not square with Christian justice. They are concealed in the spacious commonplaces we hear on every hand from the lips of the respectable to lull us into accepting conventional ideals instead of thinking out the demands of the always unconventional Master whose we are. They meet us in the guise of strangers—new thoughts or new methods—only to prove old settlers in the aging pagan world from which as new creatures in Christ we must separate ourselves. And always their power lies in their ingratiating appeal to our wisdom: "Use your common sense. Look at our clothes, taste our food. What would you have more convincing?" There is not a situation which does not require all the head we possess *plus* in order to be wisely handled. A routine decision in our work, an everyday household arrangement, a matter-of-course letter, a casual remark to some acquaintance, a talk with a friend —in these are the trivial deflections that get a man's life off its Christian tracks, and send him down some siding into the surrounding heathenism, or bumping to disaster on the roadbed. And is it any easier to find and keep to the will of God our present-day communities than in ancient Canaan?

Life is constituted thus difficult and complicated in order that we may be driven to preserve close and continuous fellowship with our wise God. A Father, who knows infinitely more than the maturest of His children, is indispensable. He may never be outgrown but grown up to. He is no court of last resort when all lower tribunals fail us. He is no safety brake to be applied when our checks and restraints prove futile, and we are headed for certain destruction. If we needed Him only in emergencies, He would no doubt be a most precious but a seldom sought Friend. We may well be thankful for crises that compel us to seek Him, but when once we have found Him, He wishes us to remain with Him.

⌁ SATISFYING WHICH HUNGER?

Consider the meaning of Jesus' first temptation in the wilderness. One hesitates to try to interpret it, for we live and think on a level so far below His; but we must try to catch a glimpse of what is passing in His mind. We may imagine Him thinking: "God's Representative! . . . with measureless powers! . . . I am hungry. . . ." Recall Jesus' hearty enjoyment of life's good things, His keen appreciation of beauty, His craving for friendship. "If I be God's Son, why not gratify My natural longings? Why this ideal of a Servant destined to be lonely and misunderstood, cut off from the fulness of life? Have I strength for any such career?" And the tempting voice was no merely selfish appeal. He who could picture unemployed men eating out their hearts in the market-place in unwilling idleness and who could sketch a comfortably reared boy so ravenous in the far country as to long for the swine's husks, looked out on the inhabitants of the conquered province of Syria, bled by grasping tax-farmers, and felt keenly their abject poverty. "Why not devote myself, with my unusual capacities, to men's first wants? Let me at least get these people well nourished, and show them the friendliness of God in a way that they can all understand; then they will recognize the caring heart of God in me, and let me lead them on to something further." And into His mind came the austere account of Israel's first days of freedom with hunger in the wilderness: "Man shall not live by bread alone, but by every word that proceedeth out of the mouth of God. . . ." "This overwhelming mission assigned me will bring with it strength as I seek to fulfil it. And if I serve men with vision and justice and redeemed consciences, they will *live,* and find the means to keep themselves alive."

Is this a struggle of the past? If anything, is it not even more acute in our time with our emphasis upon physical health and comfort as the basis of life? Is not every American child impressed that, whatever he may accomplish, he must get on and be well-off? Is it not graven upon the mind of the nation that, fine as it is to serve mankind in altruistic fashion, its first concern is to be prosperous, to commit itself to no measure which might lower its standards of living, to become involved in no entanglements which would raise its taxes, or curtail the ease of its people? Individually and nationally, do we not say to the Lord our God: "We are kindly and generous, and pride ourselves on having goodwill towards all men; but we stipulate that in showing it, there shall be no interference with good business conditions, and no abridgement of the ample scale upon which Thou hast graciously accustomed this chosen people to live"? It is hardly bread that is in our minds; that we associate with starving Russians or refugees in the Near East. We are on the cake-and-ice-cream standard. Small wonder, then, that the cross of Christ puzzles us, and we have difficulty in understanding why He resolved to undergo it! The thought of a servant nation, bearing the woes and sins of others, the thought of ourselves as involved in the iniquities of men and under obligations to offer ourselves to end them, does not occur to us. We have unconsciously reversed the order of the Lord's Prayer, and ask first, "Give us this day our daily bread," then, "Thy kingdom come, Thy will be done." It is not surprising that poorly paid callings, no matter how useful, do not capture the attention of our ablest college students; not surprising that we have the unenviable reputation abroad of single-hearted devotion to our dollars. Underneath we are aware of something else by which men and nations live, and there is as much idealism in us as in other peoples; but we are conscious of a vast gulf between ourselves and this Son of man, who unbares His thought to us, and shows Himself resolved on a course which will lead Him whither we take admirable precautions not to be led.

✍ THE BOUNDLESSNESS OF GOD

There are peaks of vision whence God lets us see what He wills for us. Have we climbed them, and looked at our life with Him? There is holy ground where a man kneels and commits his way to a Wiser Guide, and finds his paths directed. Do we know His leading? There is a fountain for sin and for uncleanness, and the hosts of the redeemed have visited it, and come away born anew. Have we taken the soil and smirch of life and the weakness and disease of our own wills to it for cleansing? There is a place of power to which ordinary folk have gone, and come away to do extraordinary things. Have we ever sought this reinforcement? There is a spring of living water, of which tired and disheartened men and women drink, and lift up their heads in courage and indomitable hope. There are outlooks whence the eyes of the heart have sight of the splendour of a diviner day, and where the beauty of the Lord comes upon and transfigures wistful spirits, and ever after this their faces are "lit with their loving and aglow with God." This—and we have not begun to circle the spiritual globe or to map out the travels of the soul and its amazing discoveries—this is the goodness of the Lord in the land of the living. It is inexhaustibly rich, as each generation bears witness, and it invariably suggests other and fairer goals of our journeying where "eye hath not seen nor ear heard nor hath it entered into the heart of man to conceive the things which God hath prepared for them that love Him." But only those who taste and see are sure, and can make others want to taste and see.

Those who have read Dr. George A. Gordon's auto-biographical volume must have noticed the letter Mrs. William James wrote him, when she asked him to conduct the funeral service for her husband:

> I want you to officiate at the funeral as one of William's friends, and also as a man of faith. That is what he was; I want no hesitation or diluted utterance at William's funeral.

An eighteenth-century Scottish divine, a man of deep personal devoutness, Thomas Halyburton, said to the physician who was attending him in his last illness: "There is a reality in religion, Doctor; but this is an age that hath lost the sense of it." Ours is an age that feels for and craves the sense of it. Thoughtful folk have been faced with the alternative: "Unless I believe to see the goodness of the Lord in the land of the living"—and the alternative makes us shudder. But the goodness of the Lord is real only to those who venture upon it utterly, use it as the clue to life, the stimulus to serve, the stay on which they rest in tranquil confidence.

✒ INVINCIBLE IDEALS

Visions fire men's imaginations, kindle their hopes, en-list their loyalties, and call out their resolves. Let imagination, prompted by Christian love, play upon all the situations and circumstances of life you confront. Dream what a household's ways, a school's studies, a factory's work, a farm's life, a community's pleasures, a nation's influence, a church's ministry, would be like were it controlled by such love as was divinely commended to us on Calvary. Count no time wasted spent in building such castles in the air. Suppose they are in the air; that is where they should be, aloft and conspicuous; and gradually the foundations of many generations can be raised up to give them solid and substantial substructure. Such gleaming air-castles on the horizon are of more actual worth to humanity than all the skyscraping steel edifices that house its present business. Nothing is comparable in value to the ideal made concrete in vision. Men must see what may be before they determine that it is so good that they will venture their all to make it come true.

> *One man with a dream, at pleasure,*
> *Shall go forth and conquer a crown;*
> *And three with a new song's measure*
> *Can trample a kingdom down.*

PRAYERS

God of our life, who meetest us on every hand in the beauty and bounty of nature, in the love which binds us to the living and the dead, in glimpses of truth, in the calls of duty, in our experiences of gladness and of grief, through the faith of Thy servants of old and the devotion of believers at our side, in the quiet thoughts of our own hearts and in the aspirations of a worshipping company, draw aside the veils and set our spirits face to face with Thee.

Thine eyes are in every place, for Thy thought and love go out to all men. Send our minds and hearts abroad until we too feel our kinship with the world-wide brotherhood of Thy children and crave for all, as for ourselves, health of body, education that frees from superstition and ignorance, liberty to think and live as sons and daughters of God, a chance to work and a chance to rest, a conscience made sensitive by the ideals of Christ and a soul that trusts and serves Thee in His Spirit.

The, live.

O Father, whose loving kindnesses have been ever of old, who art faithful to the faithless and good to the faithful beyond all their desert, deliver us from changeful minds unstayed on Thee, from selfish desires which close every window of heaven in our souls, from hearts darkened by passing shadows and unsunned by heavenly calm, and make us attentive, thoughtful and quiet before Thee.

We pray for those whom Thou hast given us to love and to be loved by, for little children, for men and women warmed or chilled in spirit by the atmosphere we create, for countless lives unknown to us but so linked with us in the web of existence that our fidelity to duty means life to them and our carelessness loss. For their sakes sanctify us.

We pray for our comrades in toil and pleasure, for the companions of our hearts and the sharers of our faith, for any who look to us for guidance and for those whom we unwittingly influence for good or ill. For their sakes ennoble us.

We pray for the sick and sad and lonely, for any who feel their lives wasted or their work futile or their spirits starved, that Thy fulness in Christ may be opened to them.

And we bless Thy name for all who through the ages have sought truth and wrought righteousness and fought the good fight of faith, who being dead live on in the principles

and convictions of the world and who themselves are the enriching citizens of Thine eternal Kingdom. Take the veil
from our hearts and join us in one communion with them
now, and forever, through Him who is the King of saints,
Jesus Christ, our Lord.

The Grace of Thankfulness

꿍 A SURE WAY TO GOD

The ladder of thoughtful thankfulness is the surest way to the presence of the Father of our Lord Jesus Christ. Whatever the situation before us, first thank God, then face the circumstances—sometimes tragic like Calvary— sure of His gracious companionship. Men and women thus thankful feel obliged to God, and obliged to give His world and all His children a vast deal more for which to be thankful.

꿍 BEING GRATEFUL EVEN ON GREY DAYS

We dare not put on blinders to grim and hideous circumstances in a world of pain and injustice and misery. But it is nonetheless a world where gratitude for life is instinctive. Men who try to see life steadily and see it whole remain thankful. Robert Louis Stevenson, struggling with tuberculosis, is grateful to the Powers that be and marvels that they use him so well. Charles Lamb, with an insane sister who has murdered her mother in one of her temporary seizures, writes to a friend:

> Some have hinted, one man has prest it on me, that she should be in perpetual confinement. What she hath done to deserve this, or the necessity of such an hardship, I see not, do you? I am starving at the India House, hear seven o'clock without my dinner, and so it has been and will be almost all the week. I get home at night o'er-wearied, quite faint—and then to cards with my father, who will not let me enjoy a meal in peace. But I must conform to my situation, and I hope I am, for the most part, not unthankful.

How comely such gratitude seems! And by being thankful does not Lamb keep his own sanity, hold fast his faith, and lift himself out of a valley of shadows into Divine sunlight? "I hope I am, for the most part, not unthankful." There's a man really ascending out of life at its grimmest and darkest into the presence of God.

And how comely such gratefulness makes him. One cannot help admiring a man who writes a letter like that. No wonder Charles Lamb remains a lovable figure in our literary history. There are few more ugly traits than those which are described by certain adjectives compounded of the noun "self"—self-centered, self-conscious, self-sufficient, self-pitying, self-satisfied. Against all these thankfulness is a sure preventive. To sit down and think on life and to realize that its best has come to us, and that even when its worst has also come, its best still keeps coming—the loveliness of earth and sky, the heritage of the wise and good, the ongoings of an interesting age in which we have a part, the trust and affection of friends, the exhaustless inspirations of Christ—and then to recognize our indebtedness, and be grateful, is to be saved from conceit, and pride and boastfulness and the myriad hideous forms of selfishness. Grateful men feel obliged, and this makes them fit members of society, comely citizens of the Beloved Community, harmonious with the life of the city of God.

✑§ KEEPING A STOUT HEART

Most of us find some whom it is difficult for us to get on with—members of our families, fellow-students, instructors, associates in various relations, persons against whom we cannot seem to help being prejudiced. Among St. Paul's correspondents there were those who were suspicious of him and those who cordially disliked him. Some viewed him as a renegade from the faith of his fathers; others thought him a corrupter of the faith he had espoused; others again imputed to him commercial motives or called him proud or tricky or domineering, or what not. Few have had a more troublesome past to live down or harsher things said of them. Paul might easily have become embittered and vitriolic. Only one of his letters explodes like a volcano—the letter to the Galatians, in which he used such expressions as "O foolish Galatians, who did bewitch you?" and indulged in words too coarse to be frankly translated. And the letter to the Galatians is the sole letter in which he does not first thank God for those to whom he is writing.

To get ourselves in hand—feelings, temper, tongue, pen —it is a wise rule to give thanks before we allow ourselves to speak or write to those who rouse us or seem to us problems. Let us run over in our minds difficult persons with whom we have to do, and thank God for their good qualities, difficult tasks that confront us and thank God for trusting us in hard situations, difficult ordeals through which we have to pass, and thank God for risking us on the high places of the field, difficult lonelinesses and losses to which we must accustom ourselves, and thank God for His presence in the valley of shadows and for the education given us in it as comforters. "First I thank my God." We shall deal with those who puzzle or vex us more justly; we shall handle our work more honorably; we shall go through our strains more courageously.

You may recall a letter which Stevenson, an invalid at Bournemouth, sent to William Archer, berating him for some pessimistic views of life:

> I used myself to rage when I saw sick folk going by in their Bath-chairs; since I have been sick myself, I have found life, even in its rough places, to have a property of easiness. That which we

suffer ourselves has no longer the same air of monstrous injustice and wanton cruelty that suffering wears when we see it in the case of others. So we begin gradually to see that things are not black, but have their strange compensations, and when they draw towards their worst, the idea of death is like a bed to lie on. I should bear false witness if I did not declare life happy. . . . I feel kindly to the Powers that be; I marvel that they should use me so well.

There is a man first thanking God, thanking Him where most would see little for which to be grateful, and by that religious attitude handling life with splendid sanity and contagious bravery.

We live in a world that is baffling. It cannot be otherwise since it is so big and we so small. But men, who like Paul in the first century and Stevenson in the nineteenth have gone to school to the Master of faith, acquire His secret and know how to live appreciatively: "First, I thank my God through Jesus Christ."

◅§ WHAT IS "REALISM"?

In revolt against the sentimentalism of the nineteenth century, the first quarter of the twentieth has shown a passion for belittlement. Patriotic Americans used to be proud of their nation. They saw halos about the heads of its founders and leaders. They wrote its history as an epic of freedom and justice. They lauded its democratic institutions as open doors to opportunity and progress. They pictured the land as a melting-pot where folk of many origins were transmuted into that desirable product—American citizens. From ocean to ocean and from Maine to Florida they saw Old

Glory waving over God's own country. That was the age of naive self-complacency. But current biography not only strips off the halo but parades every weakness and devotes pages to any sordid or shady episode it can unearth. History is almost exclusively the description of economic factors which made people act as they did. Our institutions are shown to be clever contrivances of the "haves" to prevent the "have-nots" from ousting them from their possessions. Our land is a series of Gopher Prairies and Zenith Cities, through which runs monotonous Main Street from the Atlantic to the Pacific, and upon it a ceaseless procession of childish, empty-pated, lascivious and hypocritical Babbitts drive their cars to no destination in particular. This is "the land of the free and the home of the brave" as biographers, historians, novelists and magazine writers portray it, often very cleverly.

But our contemporary realists are no truer interpreters than were the sentimentalists of one or more generations ago. They have lost a sense of proportion. Cynicism never gives fair estimates, nor can it ever mend matters for us. Our current writers are leaving God out of their pictures; or if they introduce Him, it is only to convict His devotees of insincerity and to make God Himself as futile or incredible. But religion supplies the background against which things stand out in their proper dimensions. First thank God—this is the right start for biography and history and the interpretation of contemporary life. We must be honest in that for which we thank God, and honest in that which we go on to say of defects and mistakes and wrongs. But this is both the just and the effective approach. If a man has something to tell you in a letter which is going to force you to wince, it makes a world of difference whether he writes to you appreciatively. We will receive almost anything from one who is giving thanks to God for us. We are assured that he will be fair and that his criticisms are born of a sincere desire to better us. And there is much in the figures of our national past, in our history and institutions, and in the America of today for which we can justly utter a hearty "Thank God." Well, let us do it, and then in the light of God look frankly at our problems and deal with them forthrightly.

✑ HOW GIVING THANKS INCREASES FAITH

Thankfulness is a secret of vigorous faith. Paul's world wore quite as godless a look as ours. His confidence in its control by the Father of Jesus Christ had ups and downs. Itemizing things for which to be grateful is the surest method of recovering one's sense of God's reality. The poet Wordsworth once wrote to his friend, Sir George Beaumont: "Theologians may puzzle their heads about dogmas as they will, the Religion of Gratitude cannot mislead us, I look abroad upon Nature, I think of the best part of our Species, I lean upon my Friends, and I meditate upon the Scriptures—especially the Gospel of St. John—and my creed rises up of itself, with the ease of an exhalation, yet a fabric of adamant." When William Wilberforce was discouraged by the opposition to his efforts to abolish the traffic in slaves and by the apathy of those whom he counted on to stand by him, we find him retiring sometimes to keep a day of humiliation, but often to keep a day of thanksgiving. He would sit down and carefully set in order public and private causes for gratitude. He was particularly explicit in his list of personal reasons for thankfulness— reasons from the way in which his life had been led, from his family affections, from his friends, from his own experiences. And as he looked at the contents of his cup, he found it running over, and what he lists in his diary ends with exclamations of praise to a gracious God. It may not

be a road which will take one out of skepticism into
assured trust; it is certainly a path out of little faith—the
faith that forgets God and leaves Him out of our calculations—into robust confidence. That vigorous faith is the
victory that overcometh the world.

Scan the national horizon today, and set down promising
circumstances—the leadership our country is taking, the
far-reaching and definite proposals it is setting before the
nations, the manifest popular backing for advances towards
preparations for peace only, and that list can be vastly
enlarged. Scan the industrial situation, and itemize points
for which Christians should be thankful—continued rest-
lessness where fraternal relations are manifestly lacking,
the growing demands that all participants in the work of
the world hold themselves as servants of the commonwealth,
the measure of success in the occasional enterprise where a
serious attempt is made to establish comradelike relations
among all who share with understanding, with capital or
with the labor of head or hand, the increasing desire among
all classes of the community to arrive at disarmament in
industry so that wasteful and frequently bloody industrial
strife shall be rendered impossible—and there is much in
the industrial situation for which Christians can be grateful. Scan the outlook for the Church of Christ to detect
hopeful signs—the development of a world-wide mind in
people fitting them to face a Gospel to be given to every
creature, the general feeling that we have let our material
advances outstrip our spiritual progress, the thoughtfulness
which is tracing back both international and industrial
irritations to wrong motives and ideals and which looks for
some power that can change hearts and that opens wide a
door for the everlasting Gospel, the undamaged condition
in which the Figure of Christ emerges from all our catas-
trophes when almost everything else is smashed, giving
Him an added appeal who is the same yesterday, today and

forever; and while the Church of Christ is criticised and condemned, sometimes justly, oftener ignorantly, the thing she is here to do is more manifestly wanted than ever, and the Christ she has to offer more gloriously adequate with His unsearchable riches, so that every follower who has the chance to serve Him ought to be down on his knees with gratitude for the privilege. Finally, let each man of us scan his own circumstances for causes of gratitude. Take the worst—the saddest occurrence of the year, the bitterest cup that was pressed to our lips, the most tragic loss—and as one looks it over there are always mitigating elements, things that might easily have been far more distressing, circumstances connected with it for which one cannot help being sincerely thankful. And alongside the occasional tragedy place the blessings which have come to every one of us—home happinesses, love and friendship pouring their unstinted joys, far more kindnesses shown us than we have merited, the discipline of life, God's forgiveness and His healing grace.

PRAYERS

Eternal Father, the dwelling-place of Thy children in all generations, before whom stand the spirits of the living and the dead, we thank Thee for the heritage of them that fear Thy name and for the noble succession of the faithful in which Thou hast set us: for all who throughout the ages have done justly, loved mercy and walked humbly with Thee, for the wise of every land who have led mankind into truth.

More especially we bless Thee for the Gospel of Thy grace in Jesus Christ, for apostles who have spread it throughout the earth, for martyrs who have testified their faith by their blood, for scholars who have interpreted it to the mind of successive generations, for pastors and leaders of Thy Church who have counselled young and old in the way of Christ, and for countless men and women, learned and simple, in whom His Spirit has lived and wrought through the centuries. And we remember those through whom He came to us, the guides of our childhood and the inspirations of our later years, comrades in the service of Thy kingdom who being dead yet speak unto us, beseeching thee to keep us loyal to the trust they have committed to us, to enable us to pass it on with increase to them who shall come after and to grant us enriching communion with them in Thee, both now amid earth's shadows, and forever in that life where they see eye to eye and know as they are known, through Jesus Christ our Lord.

O God, with whom dwell the spirits of just men made perfect, we praise Thee for the upright, the brave, the believing of all generations, for those who by word or work or life have been witnesses of Christ; more especially for those whose memories abide in our hearts, kindred and friends whose faces we behold no more but whose love is ever with us, the teachers and companions of days gone by, and every soul who has brought us correction, sympathy, and hope, and made Thee more real and more dear to us; and we pray that we may feel ourselves fellow-citizens with them of the city of God, and kindred in the household of faith; and walking worthily of their high and holy company in the days of our pilgrimage, may find our home with them in Thee, through Jesus Christ, their Lord and ours.

Christian Purpose
for Our Corporate Life

Are folkways fixed? Is the world doomed to remain worldly? Recall the rapidly shifting picture in the last few hundred years of the trafficways on this continent. What would Peter Minuit think of the island of Manhattan he bought from the Indians in 1626 could he look it over from the top of the Empire State Building? How George Washington would stare at the beautiful bridge, spanning the Hudson, which now bears his name! No doubt the motives of the men and women who walk the streets and cross the bridges and travel the motor highways of our time are not so markedly different from those of the farmers and traders and sailors to be found in the first settlements. It takes longer and is much more difficult to alter the motives of men than to change the routes of traffic. But it can be done; it has been done. Christianity stands or falls by the truth of its Gospel that God in Christ remakes men. And remade men blaze and steadfastly pursue new folkways.

A professor in a western college has published from contemporary documents a narrative of the movement of some fifty thousand immigrants across two thousand miles of prairie and desert and mountain, entitled *The Forty-Niners*. The leaders of the companies which got through to California concerned themselves with keeping up their people's spirits. When these were upheld, physical health, kindly personal relations among men thrown together under circumstances where it was easy to get on each other's nerves and become quarrelsome, sane judgment in the treatment of their beasts and in their facing of dangers and difficulties, could be looked for. It is a great story of folkways among an uprooted host moving towards new conditions—the same overland trail for fifty thousand, but it became one trail to the hopeful and quite another to the panicky, the homesick, the downhearted.

It may not be easy to extract optimism for mankind out of the particular stretch of human history we are now travelling. But men have walked as bleak and far bleaker stretches before us, and Christian men have walked them jubilantly. They did not draw their confidence out of the contemporary picture. Think of trekking along week after week over a dusty and rutted trail, with alkalied horses and cattle dying at the roadside, with frequent debris and signs of wreckage telling grim tales of failure, passing at times a party headed eastwards who had given up in despair, with now and again a stark mad person, for whom the strain of the enterprise had ended in mental collapse, footing it homeward. Is that unlike the picture of mankind today seeking the gold of international peace, the gold of economic security with work assured every worker and a return to provide a decent livelihood for himself and his dependents, the gold of an abundant life for human beings of all races in friendly intercourse enjoying together a world which belongs to all of us?

But what of the spirit in which we journey—we older folk and those about to take our places as leaders of spiritually migrant humanity? Do we really believe in the living God? Do we believe that God was in Christ reconciling the folkways to His way and hath committed unto us the *Word* of reconciliation?

There are many confusing voices; was there ever an age more wistful for a clear, sure word? The Christian Gospel is that the Most High Lord of heaven and earth spoke frankly in Jesus; and that this frankness of God in Jesus contains the requisite wisdom for the problems of every succeeding age. Paul, who tried to use this wisdom for his day with folkways different from those which Jesus had trod in Galilee, spoke of this wisdom as "hid in Christ." He did not mean that it is purposefully concealed from us, but stored up in His figure and to be applied with thoughtful effort and all the current knowledge with which our time supplies us. In Christ is "the word of reconciliation," which, if rightly spoken, can take and alter these folkways into highways for our God and His companionable sons and daughters.

That word *is committed* to you and me. There are two ways of receiving such a trust in a time like ours: the whimpering way and the exultant way. We may look about us at the difficulties and within us at the meagerness of our resources, and keep talking of the hopelessness of the task. Or we may look up, and say: "Now God be thanked who has matched us with this hour."

Among the Forty-Niners in the worst spot near the Humboldt River one company was bickering whether to move forward or lay up for a day. An old chap, nicknamed "Indiana," had fallen behind, but he got a passing wagon to carry a message to his outfit:

> Go on partners, go on. I've sent on my vote for
> to march ahead *whether I ever catch up or not.*

⊷§ PRESENT-DAY POLYTHEISM

It seems a truism that we have outgrown the pagan interpretation of our spiritual home, which saw the unseen world about us peopled with a discordant company of many gods—the world upon which Homer's poems look out, where one divinity favors the Greeks and another the Trojans, where three jealous goddesses contend for a prize, where one deity is the defender of Achilles and another the protector of Ulysses. But is it not a fact that we trust and follow one spirit in our homes and another in our

179

business dealings, one spirit in our patriotism and another in our attitude to men of another race, one spirit in our practical affairs and another in our church? Unconsciously, we slip back into a crude polytheism. We do not feel that the same spirit is to be relied on and obeyed in every sphere of life and in all our relations with our fellow-men. We do not believe that the same motives and incentives which can be trusted to make a satisfactory home can be used in the remaking of a world. Instead of holding with the seers of Israel in the unity of God, we are back among the rival deities who filled the Greek Olympus. Judaism still has its essential message to deliver to the world: "Hear, O Israel, the Lord our God is one." Christianity rests upon that parent faith. The New Testament as truly as the Old testifies to one God, of whom and through whom and unto whom are all things. If we worship God as love in our homes, we cannot adore Him as force in our international relations, nor as self-interest in our commercial affairs, nor as impersonal energy in control of nature. He is one and the same everywhere and always. If to know Him as Father and to be His fearless, confident and devoted children is true religion for you and me, and is not too good to be our religion, then we cannot think that to know Him as less than Father and to be frightened, fatalistic and unhoping is true religion for any of our fellow-mortals, in Asia or Africa, and it is good enough religion for them. Our spiritual home is one God, in whom we dwell with our nearest and dearest, and with men of other races and climes, one God in whom we worship and do our daily business and form our opinions and have our friendships, in whom we find a unified life, all of a piece and all of it divine.

❧ THE HIGHER WISDOM

Were Solomon to return among us, we might prize very highly his advice about our public questions. How interesting it would be to watch his keen intellect focussing itself upon the problems that confront us at this hour in international relations, in our industries, in our social difficulties! How eagerly we should scan the interview with this most distinguished visitor some enterprising reporter would secure for his paper! We suspect that Solomon would find a great many people hailing his astute conclusions with the rapturous praises of the somewhat exuberant Queen of Sheba: "Behold, the half was not told me." But if Jesus of Nazareth and of Calvary were to come among us, and tell us His mind on our present situation, were to recall us to His course of sacrificial service, were to advise us to follow invariably the love that beareth, believeth, hopeth, endureth all and never faileth, would His counsel be greeted as wisdom? Solomon is here, in the sense that his point of view is still widely represented by leading men who seem to have his knack of getting on in the world, and are accepted as knowing the world. Jesus is here, in the consciences of those who let His Spirit lead them, and very often they are accused of not knowing the world because their course in it takes them to a cross. But the world is not irresponsive to the cross. Solomon's magnificence has long since turned to dust, and his splendors have faded from men's memories. Doubtless they might seem relatively tawdry splendors today, and his riches hardly an appreciable sum in the vaster amounts with which we moderns figure. But the cross still abides with its living challenge to men's consciences. It has lost none of its lustre, and we still look back from our wealthiest treasures of inspiration and speak with astonishment of "the unsearchable riches of Christ." There are not many who venture to call Jesus a fool. But it takes unlimited courage and unbounded faith to follow His wisdom. Solomon's worldly sagacity is very appealing. It seems so entirely sensible. In a world of force, let us be prepared with adequate arms. In a world of competition, let us know how to outdo our rivals. In a world of fraud, let us not be too trusting. In a world not yet ideal, let us temper our idealism with prudence, and keep on the safe side. Solomon does not counsel Calvary. There is not the faintest suggestion of the cross in his luxurious and magnificent and prosperous career. True he enslaved his people, levied huge taxes to keep up his army and navy, and left a kingdom which went to pieces after his death. "A greater than Solomon is here." Dare we risk with Him the venture for ourselves and our land of bearing the cross, convinced that it is "the wisdom of God"?

✎§ THE POWER OF A GREAT HOPE

We often speak of America as "a land of hope," and such it has proved to many millions, from the company who landed at Plymouth Rock to the latest arrivals at Ellis Island. Probably there is more optimism among us than among any other people on the earth. A good deal of it is the easy buoyancy of spirit that comes with prosperity and the sense of a large unused bank account in our national resources. Much of it is a cheap cheerfulness which fools itself by ignoring sinister signs or by putting a good label on that to which it does not belong. Walt Whitman expressed the attitude of a great many of his fellow-countrymen when he wrote: "My notion is, I am myself just as much evil as good, and I say there is, in fact, no evil, or, if there is, I say it is just as important to you, to the land or to me as anything else." Further, much of our optimism is sheer thoughtlessness. We happen to be fairly comfortable, and we do not look ahead or bother ourselves with the question: What is in store for our country?

Israel's history enforces the lesson of the all-importance of a confident expectation. Hope chained that many-times dying people to national life. And from the pilgrims down American patriots have had mighty hopes for this country. As in Israel's case the hopes have varied with the situation in the successive generations. What the hundred and two exiles on the *Mayflower* hoped for is one thing; what we with a broad and wealthy land stretching from ocean to ocean and inhabited with more than a hundred and fifty million self-reliant people hope for is another thing. Paul wished to link the hope of Israel with the figure of Christ, and chain these patriotic Jews to that. Have you and I connected all our hopes for our country with the Spirit of Christ? Jesus took the anticipations of Israel's prophets and purged them. Sit down with your Bible and read again what an Isaiah, a Micah, a Jeremiah, an Ezekiel, a Joel, hoped for, and then think of the Kingdom Jesus proclaimed, and it will be clear how thoroughly He cleansed the hope of selfish and narrow and cruel elements and affirmed with indomitable confidence the coming of everything that was good enough to be true with His God. Take our patriotic dreams for America—America's influence on Europe, on Asia, on South America; America's part in bringing to pass international fellowship, in achieving hearty commercial and industrial cooperation, in supplying every part of the earth with the knowledge, the ideals and the convictions essential to make ours a sane, just and believing world —and let the light of Christ play on those dreams until it burns away every arrogant, grasping, unfraternal factor in them. Then let the faith of Christ affirm that these dreams are not too good to be true, with His Father on the throne

—yes, that anything less would be unworthy of such a God, and that these things can and will all come to pass, if we let this hope chain us to a loyal comradeship with our Father and to obedience to His will. Then think of the kind of'citizenship to which we are chained, to what manner of dedicated thinking and living we are bound. The present you and I can make to our country is to commit ourselves, saying: "For because of the Christian hope of America I am bound with this chain."

❧ NEWNESS OF LIFE IN CHRIST

It is true that foundations we have known are being destroyed, and meanwhile the righteous must not only go on being righteous: they must seek to be more righteous. That super-righteousness is what the generations of faithful souls before us have discovered in Jesus. Shallow critics of Christianity are calling it hopelessly outmoded because it attempts to tie mankind to the "Jesus-stereotype," and so bind the life of the present to a first-century pattern. Jesus never asked disciples to copy Him, but to follow Him; and always that has kept them working out for themselves new forms in which to utter their convictions, new ideals of conduct, and new social-institutions in which to express their consciences.

When an orchestra today renders a work of some seventeenth-or-eighteenth-century composer, they do not reproduce exactly the symphony as he wrote and gave it. The instruments in their hands are different from the instruments in the hands of musicians then. The music has to be interpreted, if you will, *re-created,* each time it is rendered. But the composer's melodies and harmonies abide and are the inspiration of the present-day rendering. Nor does the repetition of the works of Bach and Handel hold back the development of modern music. Their words stimulate and keep to the highest standards of art fresh compositions.

The figure of Jesus is no confining mould cramping the righteous of our time in a first-century pattern. Looking to Him has never meant looking backward and finding progress blocked by Him, but looking upward and seeing a huge advance required to bring current life anywhere near His level. To His followers age after age He is the supreme incentive to go forward. He shames us with things as they are about us and within us. He stings us to become different with the novelty of His mind. He empowers us with the faith that the good in Him which so masters and moves us is not just in a figure of the past—a Galilean who lived and died long ago—but is also the good in God, the good which binds all souls together in one loyal commonwealth, the good which rules sun and moon and stars of light and towards which the whole creation moves. The righteous of today, with modern instruments in their hands, must re-create for this generation the music of His life and cross. On such faith and hope and love society can rest as on the sure foundations of the living and eternal God.

☙ WHEN "PATRIOTISM" BECOMES AN IDOL

No people on earth were more truly patriotic than the Germans of the last hundred years, and their devotion to the Fatherland led them to superb achievements in education, in industrial development, in municipal government, in care for social well-being. Their moral downfall was the more tragic. And their type of patriotism which proved so disastrous to them and to the world was not theirs only. In the *Outline of History* it has been written: "In the thirteenth and fourteenth centuries the general population of Europe was religious and only vaguely patriotic; by the nineteenth it had become wholly patriotic. In a crowded English or French or German railway carriage of the later nineteenth century it would have aroused far less hostility to have jeered at God than to have jeered at one of those strange beings, England or France or Germany. To these things men's minds clung, and they clung to them because in all the world there appeared nothing else so satisfying to cling to. They were the real and living gods of Europe." And H. G. Wells continues in a parenthesis: "(Yet in the background of the consciousness of the world, waiting as the silence and moonlight wait above the flares and shouts, the hurdy-gurdys and quarrels of a village-fair, is the knowledge that all mankind is one brotherhood, that God is the universal and impartial Father of mankind, and that only in that universal service can mankind find peace, or peace be found for the troubles of the individual soul)."[3] Until the patriot weds his land to the God of the spirits of all flesh, until he thinks of her only in thoughts which include the God and Father of Jesus Christ, his patriotism is a pagan sentiment.

✍§ GOD'S COMPULSION TOWARD JUSTICE

No perfect plan will be devised for the re-ordering of the economic life of our race. Were a plan forthcoming which would appear satisfactory today, it would require revision tomorrow, for circumstances are ever shifting in this always changing human society. But Christians must insist that urban and rural slums in this wealthy country, and slum peoples in a world provided with abundance and knit together now by means of communication, are not God's will and are therefore not to be tolerated. Changes may be

[3] Copyright by Professor G. P. Wells and used with his kind permission.

uncomfortable for many of us, but changes in the interest of justice are always good for character. It is peculiarly the duty of Christians with a larger outlook on God's interest in His whole world to combat the traditionalism which obstructs social change. Neither selfishness nor timidity nor sheer bafflement by the intricacies of the economic problems must induce us to draw back. That way lies perdition— a return to conditions which by their injustices breed industrial strife and international wars. "Faith is assurance of things hoped for"— assurance not in our hopes, but because those hopes faintly mirror the purposes of our righteous God.

Again circumstances, and God who speaks through circumstances, force our generation to face the mutual relations of races. We were rightly indignant at a hideous doctrine of racial superiority in Nazi minds which brought mass murders and threatened to reduce millions to a new serfdom. We know that the most potent argument in Japanese propaganda in Asia was that the white races never treat yellow or brown or black peoples as social equals. And we cannot forget that one of the chief factors which set Japan against us was a discrimination in our immigration laws against its nationals on our part. The white race has been guilty of insufferable snobbery towards other races. This seems incredible because the New Testament which we have professed to revere is so plain that in Christ barriers of race are done away. Modern biology confirms St. Paul's affirmation that God hath made of one blood all dwellers upon earth, and our educators know that a yellow or a brown or a black skin may cover a brain equal to any under a white skin. No better reading is on the "must" list for any of us than the biography of George W. Carver. That book enables us to look out on contemporary situations through the eyes and mind and sensitive feelings of a distinguished scientist and public-minded citizen and fellow-Christian with a dark skin.

It confronts us with issues which are not easily solved. There are economic complications, long-standing habits of thought and feeling, proper regard for racial integrity in order to conserve the distinctive contributions of all races, which must be thoughtfully considered. But we have been set down in a day when social usages are necessarily becoming fluid and when we must plan a world in which the majority will be non-whites and which will seem just to them; or we shall bring on some more frightful racial conflicts for the suppression of the unbearably arrogant and domineering whites, among whom Anglo-Saxon whites are glaring offenders. We dare not allow ourselves and our country to draw back into the anti-semitisms, the Jim-crowisms, the segregations, which have prevailed. These discriminations belong in the passing order which God has condemned. He sets before us in Christ His order of brotherhood long overdue. It will demand much laborious thinking; and will call for courage, tact and perseverance to enter it and take along our contemporaries. But God waits to supply these qualities. The Gospel of Christ is a rich storehouse of them. The call is for faith—assurance of things we ought to hope for because God hopes that they will come to pass.

⊷§ THE NEXT RIGHT STEP AHEAD

In a world as wicked as ours we do not face the choice of a course which is completely Christian. Our choices are between more and less Christian alternatives. Jesus Himself did not face decisions where one way was entirely to His mind. The supreme decision to die at the hands of the Romans was not His preferred way: "O My Father, if it be possible, let this cup pass away from Me." It seemed to Him an appalling course, but the best under dreadful

188

circumstances. His followers in individual choices and in the policies for our country which we support have to adopt the more Christian course in conditions where a wholly Christian course, even were we good and wise enough to discover it, is just not open to us. That most excellent way gleams from afar. Christ gives the vision of a goal; but the tragic immediate human situation rarely, if ever, allows us to use the ideally Christian way. We see the end towards which we must move—a world nearer to His and our hearts' desire, and we see more and less Christian routes which can now be pursued. The direction in which Christ sets our faces, and the discrimination between more and less Christian paths, are part of His authority over us.

And He is more even than goad and guide: He furnishes power to take the steps. Christians are always under pressure from Him. Paul put it: "Christ's love constraineth us." It is that pressure which detaches men from conceit, laziness, self-seeking, conventionality, and sends them energetically in the friendly, the courageous, the just, the believing path. It is this compulsion which has made and still makes Christians effective. It is never the thing we *may* do that we do well. If we feel we *may*, we also feel we *may not*. If it be unpleasant or tiring we manage to dodge it. It is the thing we feel we *must* do that enlists all our powers and frees us from all inhibitions. It may be disagreeable; it may arouse criticism; it may stir up lots of trouble for us; it may let us in to arduous responsibilities we long to be clear of; but from Christ "necessity is laid" on us. We must.

✑ WHAT CAN MAKE US BROTHERLY?

Even when men feel unbrotherly toward one another, God has so tied us together that without intending it we do

189

help each other. In one of his reports of the Rockefeller Foundation, its executive, Raymond Fosdick, wrote:

> An American soldier wounded on a battlefield in the Far East owes his life to the Japanese scientist, Kitasato, who isolated the bacillus of tetanus. A Russian soldier saved by a blood transfusion is indebted to Landsteiner, an Austrian. A German soldier is shielded from typhoid fever with the help of a Russian, Metchnikoff. A Dutch marine in the East Indies is protected from malaria because of the experiments of an Italian, Grassi; while a British aviator in North Africa escapes death from surgical infection because a Frenchman, Pasteur, and a German, Koch, elaborated a new technique.
>
> Our children are guarded from diphtheria by what a Japanese and a German did; they are protected from smallpox by an Englishman's work; they are saved from rabies because of a Frenchman; they are cured of pellagra through the researches of an Austrian. From birth to death they are surrounded by an invisible host—the spirits of men who never thought in terms of flags or boundary lines and who never served a lesser loyalty than the welfare of mankind.

In that sense brotherly love continues.

But what interruptions brotherly love is exposed to! Take the United Nations—and what dangers there are for misunderstandings and jealousies. Brethren are not invariably lovable. A common danger may bind them for a while; but let the danger relax and mutual antagonisms begin to play. In nations, in businesses, in churches, in communities, even in families, brethren get on one another's nerves. Things are said which might better be left unspoken. Things are felt which should not be given into. Love grows tired using its imagination to put itself inside a brother's mind to look out through his eyes and feel with his sentiment. The one hope of a decent organization of mankind after this devastating time is that brotherly love should continue.

It will be a miracle if it does; and it is the task of the Christian Church to give God the chance to have that miracle happen. Our essential duty is to hold Him before the eyes of all the brethren, so that from Him may flow the love which believeth, hopeth, endureth all and never faileth.

And such love must be as strong a passion as the righteous wrath which consumes iniquity. Anger is an energy which gets things done or gets things done away. Martin Luther confessed: "I never work better than when I am inspired by anger." "When I am angry, I can write, pray, and preach well." But when the situation which wholesomely provokes us and puts us in a fury changes, then what? How easy to sink back into apathy! Walter Bagehot spoke of "the supine placidity of civilization." It was hard for our civilized western world to rouse itself from a placidity which tolerated an appallingly bestial tyranny. We did not care about its victims because we lacked love. But love's flame which does not die down so long as odious and hurtful forces are at work must be kept ablaze when that fuel ceases. We need a burning enthusiasm in the task of recreation.

To rear the fair structure of a friendly commonwealth of all peoples on the charred surface of this war-scorched earth, brotherly love must be as ardent as the consuming fire. Only if it is at passion will it be warm enough to dissipate the chill of depressed spirits and burn through the fogs of prejudice and continue aglow with desire for the achievement of the goal despite inevitable delays and discouragements.

There is only one source whence a love which is not an

emotion only but a resolve also can be drawn—that is the cross of Christ.

✒ HEAVENLY CITIZENSHIP

The Bible closes with a city, and brotherliness in city-dwellers consists not merely in occasional personal acts of friendship, but in the vision and conscience to incarnate thought and heart into the very fabric of the city's life, so that it is responsive to any need. Men and women who can put up contentedly with the full facts of any American city are hardly those one would select as desirable inhabitants in the city of God. Patriots who are satisfied with the justice and freedom and opportunity accorded to all the dwellers in the United States, sufficiently satisfied not to be ready even at personal sacrifice for radical changes, are scarcely promising citizens for a heavenly country. Americans who are not painfully uneasy over our nation's present attitude to mankind, who have not a whole world's woes tugging at their consciences, and whose thoughts do not make daily transatlantic and transpacific voyages in sympathy and in wistfulness to bear burdens, are not likely material for that kingdom whither they come from east, west, north and south in one community. "Inasmuch as ye did it not to one of these least, ye did it not unto Me."

PRAYERS   *Wed. eve.*

O Father, whose care outruns our thought, and whose arm extends our reach, we place in Thy safekeeping those dear to us, present and absent, all whose labor promotes our well-being, any of whom we are thinking in sickness, sorrow or loneliness, self-sufficient folk who do not crave

Thy comradeship, unbelieving folk who do not believe that they or others can live as sons of the Most High.

And we also bless Thy name for all to whom throughout the ages Thou hast been Father and Friend, who have walked trustfully and usefully before Thee in the earth, and now dwell in the city of God. Keep us all our days their co-workers for Thy kingdom, schooling us to be their fellow-citizens in that life where love crucified here is forever on the throne, through Jesus Christ, their Lord and ours.

Thur. eve

God of the spirits of all flesh, who hast knit us in one bundle of life with Thy children of every tongue and kindred, grant us Thine own sympathy to rejoice with them that rejoice and weep with them that weep, that we may truly pray with and for them. Lay on our hearts the hunger of the famished, the anxieties of the fearful, the passions of the tempted, the indignation of men unjustly used, the emptiness of soul of those without God. Exalt us to know the gladness of those who increase men's knowledge, or bind up their wounds, or break their shackles or enrich their spirits. So make us in prayer and life bearers of the burdens and sharers of the joy of our brethren, through Jesus Christ, the Saviour of us all.

Fri. eve

Most High God, our Father, lift us who seek Thy face out of our shadows into Thy light, out of our selfishness into Thine all-inclusive love, out of our insufficiency into Thy strength, out of our foolish and disappointed purposes into Thy wise and blessed will, out of our distractions and fears into Thy peace. For sin give repentance, for sorrow give hope, for self-complacency give hunger and thirst after righteousness, and kindle in us a flaming passion for all things true and just and lovely and of good report.

What things we ask for ourselves we crave for the whole family of mankind, that ignorance may be lightened by education, that disease may be mastered by science, that lawlessness may give place to order, that poverty may disappear in a juster, a less wasteful, a more conscientious order.

We pray for our country, that wisdom and public spirit may be plenteously bestowed upon the President of the United States and every citizen of the republic, that our patriotism may be truly Christian, our national character dominated by the spirit of service, our land made glad throughout its length and breadth by goodwill towards all men.

We pray for Thy Church universal, that more of its sons and daughters may give its work their thought, their energy, their prayers; that it may have larger sympathy with those to whom faith is difficult and those who misunderstand the mind of Christ; that it may resolutely put away all seeming barriers of class that prevent it from being the congenial home of the lowliest and the welcome refuge of the most sin-stained, that in its teaching and work and life it may more lovingly and persuasively mirror Jesus Christ.

And in the communion of the Holy Spirit; with the spirits of just men made perfect; with the faithful of all the ages whose lives enrich the city of God; with our beloved dead who dwell in the peace and victory of Thy presence; we who still labor and battle commit ourselves to Thy guidance, Thy comradeship, through Jesus Christ our Lord.

Gracious God, who didst send Thy Son to be King of righteousness and Prince of Peace, grant that the rulers and powers of our world may be subdued to His reign, that those who have offended may repent and those who are offended forgive, and all races and nations dwell together as one family under Him, before whose judgment all stand condemned and by whose cross all may be redeemed, even Jesus Christ our Lord.

Sat. eve

Gracious Father, whose eyes are in all the earth, lead the races and nations of mankind into mutual justice and goodwill. Further those who seek to render wars impossible. Make us ashamed that when Thou hast put it in man's power to produce so plentifully for his wants, our folly and greed leave multitudes idle and impoverished. Direct with Thy counsel those in authority in this and other lands; inspire leaders in industry with wisdom to plan the world's work so that none is debarred from his share either of labor or of the results of labor; consecrate Thy Church to enthrone the mind of Christ in the consciences of all men. We ask it in the Redeemer's name.

What the Church May Be

❧ POWER FROM ON HIGH

Pentecost pictures a group of men as waiting and expecting God to take the initiative; it pictures God as coming, coming in compelling force, kindling hearts with the flame of love; it pictures men who had never been able to understand one another hearing each in his own tongue the message of a new day of God's presence among men in a Christlike brotherhood.

In a book published some years ago, an eminent British archaeologist places side by side two maps of Europe as he thinks it appeared in the glacial and in the warm periods. In the cold age the sea was at least six hundred feet higher than its present level, and man was confined to narrow peninsulas and scattered islands, and as sea-trafficking was as yet unknown, his arts deteriorated, and life became impoverished to the brutal type exemplified in the beastlike skeleton unearthed in the Neanderthal. In the warm periods there was a wide continent, with a continuous shore line from Denmark to Britain and a chain of lakes running from the Black Sea to the Atlantic, and the sea level approximately six hundred feet lower than at present. From these periods come artistic remains vastly superior to those of the glacial epochs. The difference in the map is due almost entirely to a difference in temperature. Cold means disunity and deterioration; warmth means unity and advance. Pentecost is a change in climate. To waiting, anticipating, believing men God comes, and when present He alters the registry on the moral thermometer. There is a striking rise in heart and conscience, and men find themselves mutually intelligible and bound together in hearty friendship.

Is not this the prerequisite of the unity we so crave today —international, ecclesiastical, industrial? We cannot make it; all our arduous efforts are foredoomed to confusion. We can grow it, but only in the right climate: a further opening of human life to God, a new waiting upon Him in expectant faith, a confidence that He is to be looked for from within lives believingly attached to Jesus Christ, and that given scope by those who believe in His indwelling He manifests Himself in love, the conscientious love which bears and shares and believes and hopes and never fails.

ᴥ§ WHY THE CHURCH?

Many persons in our time think that they can be disciples of Jesus without regard to the institution which represents His religion. But in fact it is the Churches which pass on the heritage of the devout generations, which supply children with training in Christian convictions and standards, which provide men and women with inspiration at every stage of their lives, and which open to them a chance to invest themselves to spread the Christian faith in their own city and land and to the ends of the earth in the worldwide propaganda of Christian missions. No church may altogether suit any man or woman. If it does, it is to be hoped that he will stay out of it; for if he comes in, he is likely to be a brake on progress. Our Lord was not wholly satisfied with the synagogue at Nazareth, where "as His custom was" He regularly attended. How dull He must have found the preaching of scribes, and how much of the service He must have felt outmoded! But He agreed heartily with the great end for which the Church existed, and His was no finicky conscience insistent upon having every item in the Church's witness please Him before He would give it His allegiance. To Him the Church was the transmitter of the Spirit and a home of the faith in which He had been brought up. To Him the Church was a necessity for the cultivation of His fullest life with God; and despite differences with those who ruled synagogue and temple, He worshipped at their side. To Him the Church furnished the chance to contribute His own spiritual gift: and synagogue and temple found Him ready to share His experience of God.

Creditor to whom we owe the Christian inheritance, aid to the Christian life, and channel to give our influence under God widest outflow and keep it streaming in the spiritual life of the race long after we are gone—this the Church is to Christians today.

The Church of His age found Jesus a troublesome member because of His criticisms of its leaders, of the products of its missionary work, of its accepted standards of a good life. And because He was provocative and disturbing, the congregation at Nazareth was enraged at Him, and the authorities at Jerusalem had Him crucified.

The peril of the Church in every age is intolerance of the innovator. When Peter had a vision from heaven bidding him broaden out and receive a new group into the Church, he replied: "Not so, Lord, for I have never." His tradition and habit were to limit God's activity. A Christian Church, with room in it for Jesus of Nazareth, must safeguard the liberty of the unsettling critic. He may seem, and sometimes he is, a fool; but even when tactless and unwise, he may be a messenger of God. Our Father employs odd agents. See that we make the Church open-minded.

❧ THE WISTFULNESS IN SEEMING UNBELIEF

A man's head may be outside the Church altogether and his wistful heart stay inside. It's an uncomfortable position, but it has been the plight of hundreds of saints; and the wistful heart should be accorded its rights no less than the skeptic head. If a man's conscience has outgrown the Church so that he chafes at its patience with intolerable conditions and its blindness to Christ's light, His place is not outside. Let him take up his cross, even if the whole Church seems the cross: his Lord did no less. If he finds the Church religiously unsatisfying, let him draw on whatever wayside fountains supply him with living water, but let him share his supplies with the Church that bore him, exactly as Jesus went straight from His new filling with the Spirit at the Jordan to the familiar synagogue in Nazareth, saying: "The Spirit of the God is upon Me" and seeking to bestow the gift of God on those at whose side He had prayed and learned since childhood. The Church is the household of faith, and one cannot sever family ties at will: they are life-long responsibilities. The Church is the native land of Christian spirits; the greatest patriots have wept bitter tears over their countries; but they never voluntarily threw off their allegiance. No, the patriot heart sounds in the song that comes from the rivers of Babylon:

> *If I forget thee, O Jerusalem,*
> *Let my right hand forget her cunning.*
> *Let my tongue cleave unto the roof of my mouth,*
> *If I remember thee not;*
> *If I prefer not Jerusalem*
> *Above my chief joy.*

The Lord's people really cannot live their lives outside the Lord's land. Many of them think they can. They assure you that they are just as good as those within its borders— a pathetic indication of complacent self-righteousness which shows that they are not very close to that towering Figure who makes all near Him feel poor in spirit. They tell you of satisfactions to their souls in the broad streams of Babylon which they contrast with the brooks of Zion in their narrow gorges. But in their serious moments they are wistful, and they are often very lonely and homesick. A young Yale graduate, some sixty years ago, when contemporary currents of thought had carried him outside the Church where he had been reared, confided in a letter to a classmate:

> For my part I long to "fall in" with somebody. This picket duty is monotonous. I hanker after a shoulder on this side and the other.

ঌ THE CHURCH'S REAL MEMBERS

If a church is an audience, then a tramp who moves about hearing distinguished preachers and tasting the choirs of various congregations hears better preaching and music than the home-body who sticks week after week in the same spot. Tramps have no burdensome obligations, but what steady member of a family circle fails to find responsibilities accumulating? Wanderers among churches, like travellers in foreign lands, are observers and feel at liberty to criticize; but a member of a household, while he tries to improve whatever he sees amiss, finds his sense of loyalty preventing his discussing his relatives. No one looks very sharply at the artistic or inartistic arrangement of a room to which he has become long accustomed; he accepts the pictures on the walls, the well-worn sofa and chairs and desk. They serve his needs, and he lives, does his work, talks with his loved ones in that homelike room. So a church ceases to be scrutinized critically by those whose spiritual life develops in its fellowship. They are well aware that other congregations excel at a hundred points, just as hundreds of homes have advantages of one sort and another over theirs; but this is their church, the home of their Christian work and faith. It gathers their affection and fastens ever more firmly their allegiance with the passing years. Say what you will about it, it is home to them.

And it is a family of faith. The kinship which holds them together is the tie which binds each to God. The service each is called to render is to establish the contact with God in the home where he lives, the business where he works, the civic life in which he shares, the pleasures in which he finds his recreation, the friends with whom he meets. Here is a group of persons all of whom are "next" and whose very presence puts the circle in which they are in touch with the Father of Jesus Christ. There is a certain amount of overlapping between our churches and other organizations; many institutions offer some of the same helpful services which the churches supply. Our distinctive task is connecting people with God through Christ. Every member of a church fulfils a function not dissimilar from that of the switch-board operator—he places a home, a social circle, a business-office, a city problem in touch with the all-sufficient Source of wisdom, strength and goodness. He belongs to the household of the faith.

And every member of a household contributes something to the family life. Our King James Version makes St. Paul say: "Now ye are the body of Christ and members in particular." It is a good old English phrase which persists in our popular parlance. You bring some friend with you to a church service, and as you are walking home he asks you: "Who was that man in your church three seats ahead of us?" "Oh," you say, "he is nobody in particular." The plain fact is that nearly seventy-five per cent of most congregations are "nobodies in particular" in its life. Suppose the answer had been: "I don't know that he holds any office, but he's one of the stand-bys. I've seen him at the teachers' meeting; he has called on me in the every-member canvass; he's a friendly soul who has an eye out for newcomers and seems to have a faculty of making people feel at home." That's "a member in particular."

৵§ ADJUSTED TO WHAT?

It is not so long since a major aim was to make the Church abreast of the times. We talked of adapting her message to current thought and fitting her work into current social trends. We did not realise that we were conforming her to this age—making her worldly. If she is to redeem an evil day, she must not voice its mind nor fit into its patterns. Her significance lies in her unique and distinctive contribution—a contribution which she derives not from the time, not from this world, but from God who has entered the world in Christ and who is always seeking to enter it and rule it by His Spirit. It is her difference from the life of the time which enables her to redeem it. No doubt she has to make her message intelligible to each generation and she must find men where they are; but it is what she brings to them which matters, and the distance she takes them from where they are towards where they ought to be.

She must not be preoccupied with the tendencies in contemporary thinking. Contemporary thinking belongs to an evil day. She must be listening to God's Word spoken once fully in Christ and being spoken to her constantly by the living Spirit. Her members must not be anxious whether they are in tune with the time; if we are, we are harmonious with an evil day. We must ask what is distinctive about us which separates us from our generation and which enables us to bring something effective to its redemption. Are we adjusted to it, or are we adjusting it to God's eternal purpose?

In her vigorous epochs the Christian Church re-fashioned the contemporary mind. See her changing the whole outlook of the old Roman world; see her re-making the barbarian tribes which her missionaries converted in the days of her expansion through Europe; see her creating new consciences in the Reformation; see her in revival after revival giving men new ideals, new scruples, new characters, new power to be different and make their day different. These great epochs were not periods when she was anxiously fitting her Gospel to the current mind. She was hearing God revealing Himself to her so compellingly that Christian minds changed and made Him dominant. Then she had something arresting to say to the time which redeemed it.

In the early 'nineties there was a movement in Britain to have the government recognize eminent men of letters. Dr. Robertson Nicoll, editor of *The Bookman*, started a discussion on the subject, and sought the view of Thomas Hardy. He replied:

> I daresay it would be very interesting that literature should be honoured by the state. But I don't see how it could be satisfactorily done. The highest flights of the pen are mostly the excursions and revelations of souls unreconciled to life, while the natural tendency of a government would be to encourage acquiescence in life as it is.

If that be true of literature, how true it must be of the Christian Church. "Acquiescence in life as it is"—that is the Church's constant temptation. She is the fellowship of souls unreconciled to life because they are at one with God in Christ, and therefore at variance with an evil day and out to redeem it.

And still another change is the passionate desire for such reunion of the Christian Church that she may present a common front to the evil day, and form an earthwide community binding in one all disciples of Jesus and giving them a sense of fellowship amid the disintegrating factors which are tearing our world to pieces.

In a part of China invaded in the 1940's, a Chinese pastor

in his humble hamlet church placed a sign upon it "Jesus' House." From the Japanese forces came several soldiers and officers to pray with him, to express, despite barriers of language partly bridged by a common alphabet, their oneness with him in Christ, and to do their utmost to protect him and his little congregation from the ravages of war. It was a small, a pathetically small, symbol of that new community which Christ builds—a community which knows no national frontiers—and which is the only hope of an else war-sundered world.

ৰ্৯ HOW WIDE IS THE CHURCH'S FELLOWSHIP?

Plainly it is the will of the Lord that every congregation seek to make its fellowship embrace all sorts and types of folk in its neighbourhood. It is the curse of many churches that their constituency is limited to one, or at most two, fairly congenial classes in the community. The emphasis upon a sociable church often means that its attendants are restricted to those who mix easily. Friendliness there must be, or the church misrepresents its friendly Lord; but how outreaching was His friendliness and what miscellaneous people it took in! Sociability must not be had at the expense of comprehensiveness—a congregation should include rich and poor, the pillars of society and those whom many societies deem outside their pale. Congregations must scrutinize their constituency to see whether they are failing to appeal to some elements. Every church is intended to be a house of prayer for all people.

Plainly, in this day of social change, it is the will of the Lord that the Church should teach and strive for greater economic justice. It is unhappily not true that her members are open minded to economic change for a fairer distribution of the benefits and burdens of the national heritage.

We pray in Christ's words: "Our Father, give us our daily bread," and know that we must take in all His children of every condition and land. But are we resolved that no willing worker shall be left unemployed, that slums, urban and rural, must be done away, and that no people anywhere shall be doomed to a slum level of existence? Churches may and should be uncomfortable places for the complacent and selfish. They must be aflame with a passion for justice. That is the fire of God's ancient prophets and of His Son whom apostles called "the Just One."

Again, it is plainly the will of the Lord that congregations concern themselves with racial tensions, which threaten the unity of the nation and may breed future conflicts. The Gospel we proclaim is clear that God has made of one blood all nations of men, and that in Christ there is neither Greek nor Jew, bond nor free. But how difficult to translate that into the arrangements of industry and to implant it in the public mind. We have rightly indicted the hideous doctrine of a superior race held by our enemies. But what shall we say of anti-Jewish, anti-Japanese, anti-Negro prejudices among ourselves? Anglo-Saxon whites almost never treat members of other races as their equals. Our arrogance and snobbery constitute a menace to the peace of the world, and, unless overcome, may well bring on a racial conflict more appalling than any previous war. There have been ominous signs in many cities of the tense feelings of our Negro fellow-citizens who find themselves discriminated against in industry, in the armed forces, in hotels, restaurants, places of entertainment, in housing, and even in the house of God where they are rarely made welcome with white fellow-worshippers.

In Ohio some years ago there was a contest in the schools of a city for the best essay on the topic: "What punishment should be meted out to Adolf Hitler?" The essay which was awarded the prize was by a Negro girl of sixteen and its main point was: "Give him a black skin, and put him down in any American community." What bitter experiences in that girl and among her kindred and friends lay behind that essay!

There is perhaps no graver peril at the moment before our land than the feeling among Negro young people, especially those with good education, that the Christian Church has failed them, that its profession of brotherhood is insincere, and that its members stand behind "Jimcrowism" and the caste system in jobs, by which certain occupations are considered open to Negroes and others are reserved for whites only.

The first great struggle in the early Church was a race issue—between Jews and non-Jews; six of St. Paul's letters deal with it, and insist that in Christ the color and race lines are done away. We who must build a new world today, in which whites will not be the majority, for we are less than a third of the total population, must see to it that its arrangements appear fair to the yellow, brown and black peoples. The Church will lose her leadership unless she stand unequivocally by her God-given Gospel and declare that any man or woman must be rated for what he or she is and can do, irrespective of color, and that such friendly relations with proper social intercourse shall unite the races that each can make its full contribution to the economic and political commonwealth and to the Church of God.

ᴇ§ A WORLD OUTLOOK

How trifling appear denominational differences among us, how irrelevant our inherited divisions, and how stupidly hampering the competitions and overlappings, in the light of the mission committed to us to make all nations Christian! When we discuss means of compassing mergers of our

209

communions, mergers long overdue, and minds become tangled in the details of traditions and hearts hold tight to accustomed usages, it is all-important that we stop our talk, and quietly recollect: "We are serving Christ and seeking to fashion forms in which His Body on earth can give witness, and offer worship, and marshal its every force to put at the disposal of Him who is at the right hand of the Lord of heaven and earth." Such recollection will banish pettiness. We must provide Christ with an inclusive fellowship of His followers, with outreaches worthy of His station on the throne of the entire world.

And such a conviction of Christ's partnership with the God and Father of the spirits of all flesh will renew the consecration of His people to their comprehensive commission. "Go ye into all the world." An insidious provincialism gets into us and confines us to narrow outlooks in planning our work for Christ. There must be a re-birth of missionary enthusiasm to place us side by side with the earnest groups in the younger Churches of Asia and Africa and with the much-tried, much-suffering groups in the older Churches of Europe in an advance movement to bring the thought of mankind under Christ's sway. No peace settlement will last without a spiritual basis, and only the faith of Christ can supply that.

We need to recapture the prospect which filled the mind of one of the most forceful ministers in this country a century and a half ago, Dr. Lyman Beecher. Looking back over his ministry he said:

> From the beginning my mind has taken in the Church of God, my country and the world as given to Christ. It is this which has widened the scope of my activity beyond the common sphere of pastoral labor.

✑ OVERCOMING DIVISIONS

How broad are we? The divisions in the Christian Church have nearly always come about because devout people could not differ and still pull together in one fellowship. There must be room in the Church for diverse types of worship, differing interpretations of the Gospel, many varieties of missionary activity, a vast range of forms of social helpfulness. We have to be large enough to allow others to express their loyalty to Christ in ways which are not congenial to ourselves and rejoice in them as fellow-workers unto the Kingdom of God.

How big-hearted are we? The Church must embody the friendliness of Jesus. Metals fuse only at high temperatures, and folk of various stations in life merge as comrades only where love is warm.

When one of the steel railway-bridges which span the Mississippi at St. Louis was nearly completed, it was discovered that the halves of the structure, built out from opposite banks, did not quite meet at the centre. An engineer was sent on to New York to consult experts, and while they and he were trying to discover where an error in the calculations had been made, he received a telegram that the heat of the midsummer sun had expanded the metal and that the two ends were together. As quickly as electricity could carry the reply, he wired: "Clamp them." Love heated to the temperature of Calvary will overcome distances of snobbishness and offishness which part folk; then in the Church's fellowship the clamping can take place.

PRAYERS

O God, whose Word spoke in the prophets and dwelt in Thy Son and has been committed to Thy Church to carry to all men, renew in Christians everywhere the sense of our trust and mission. Enable us to live richly as heirs of the faith and hope and love of Christ, that men may see that in Him we have enough and to spare. Grant us both to prize whatever spiritual riches men possess from other heritages and to share with them the Christ who comes not to destroy but to fulfil. Where Thy Church is persecuted, uphold it; where it is superstitious, enlighten it; where it is faint-hearted, embolden it; and throughout the world bind us together as one body of Christ, and fill us with His life and light and love.

And we also bless Thy name for that great company of our comrades in Christ who have passed through the earth illumining its ways with His glory, and have entered the city to which He is the unsetting sun. Make us partakers of that faith by which they wrought mightily and bore patiently in their day, that they may welcome us with Him to whose service here and there we dedicate ourselves forever.

O King of Saints, who hast through all the ages fulfilled Thy plans through faithful souls, loyal to truth, steadfast in conviction, brave for conscience sake and lovers of men, grant that as we recall that glorious succession, unknown and well-known, to whose toil and courage we owe our faith, our freedom and our ideals, we may drink of their cup of devotion to Thy will, and be baptised with their consecration to men, and in our day inspire our generation with trust in God, with passion for Thy loving justice, with enthusiasm for Thy Kingdom, with unwavering hope of its world-wide establishment, through Jesus Christ our Lord.

Almighty God, in whom is calmness and concord, heal the divisions of Thy Church which separate brethren from one another. While there are diversities of knowledge and faith, and we cannot all be of the same mind, may we be made one in loyalty to Christ and in the endeavor to enthrone Him Lord of lords. Deliver us from blindness and prejudice, from intolerance and evil-speaking, that by the charity of our temper and thought and life we may show forth the beauty and power of the religion we profess and commend it to the world, in Jesus' name.

O Lord, who hast knit us together in one household of faith, make it for all of us a large room, where minds grow in knowledge and hearts expand in sympathy, where each bears his own load and his brother's burden, where all faces turn towards the light, where no walls between souls destroy our unity in Christ, where the needs of Thy children of every race and tongue come home to our consciences, where together we know and abide in Thee, the dwelling-place of the faithful in all generations, and possess for ourselves and for the service of men unsearchable riches of our Lord Jesus Christ.

The Living Bread

THE GIVEN, AND THE RECEIVED

Here is Bread, the Bread of God which comes down from heaven and gives life.

Strange the process by which the seed, buried and giving up its life, takes on from the atmosphere, the sunlight and the soil its form, and grows! Strange the process of being cut and winnowed and ground and kneaded and passed through a hot oven to become life-sustaining as bread. Strange that a man, betrayed, denied, mocked, tortured in excruciating agonies on two beams of wood, should become the life-giving Friend of millions! Strange that with the treatment you and I accord Him—honoring and forgetting, revering and ignoring, loving and discarding—He still mysteriously draws and convinces, shames and exalts. The background against which His friendliness stands out is so dark. It always seems a night in which He is betrayed. But how the friendliness shines out! How wonderful it seems! How gripping it is! And how tenacious its hold. If we are faithless, He abideth faithful. If we despair of mankind as a whole, of so-called civilized mankind in particular with all its knowledge and culture seemingly bent on self-destruction, of certain specimens of humanity with whom we have a great deal to do and who seem to us painfully akin to Judas in their shameless unreliability or who impress us as just hopelessly stupid, above all if we are tired of and out of sorts with and utterly despondent about ourselves, here is the reminder of the Love that beareth, believeth, hopeth, endureth all and never faileth.

And the reminder by His own designing is expressed for us in bread and a cup, of which He says, "Take." The love that bears, trusts, hopes, endures and conquers is not to be produced by ourselves. It is true that you and I must do the loving, the trusting, the hoping, the enduring, just as He did, and did to the end, and goes on doing without end.

But such love is not self-originated and self-sustained in any man. Take, eat, drink. Love is the life of God. God is love. To believe, to receive, this Son of God, this strange Man of yesterday and today, this Friend who appeals and gives Himself again and again and again, is, as generations of Christians bear witness, to be lifted up to His faith, to be possessed by and to share His hope, His life.

✑ THE SOUL'S "IRON RATION"

Here is the Table of Christ with all needed supplies for that to which the Master sends us forth. There are some who will never forget the issuing of the ration on the eve of an attack—"the iron ration." It had to be compact, so that a man could carry it easily. It had to be something that would not spoil, for men went into rain and mud, heat and dust. It had to be very nourishing, for it was to sustain men in the most nerve and body exhausting strain that human beings can be called to undergo. Here is the Christian soldier's iron ration. It is compact. A college man who was thinking of the ministry as a life work asked me once whether he would have to believe "a whole lot of things." What could I do but answer: "No! Not a whole lot of things, but you must believe one thing a whole lot; and that one thing is Jesus Christ." It does not spoil. Christ lasts. Centuries have rolled by, and He is not obsolete, but seems the fresh supply of today's necessities. He has been subjected to all manner of change, as the successive generations have altered their opinions, their manner of life, their ways of doing almost everything, but He is as fitted to our time as to His own. And it is very nourishing. Who that feeds on the Bread of Life says: "It is not enough"?

> *Thou, O Christ, art all I want;*
> *More than all in Thee I find.*

❧ AS JESUS LIFTS US UP TO GOD

We often speak of Jesus as dying for us; we sometimes speak of Him rising for us; we rarely think of His ascending for us. But that was a thought in the minds of His early followers. They could not think of their Jesus as doing anything for Himself only. Wherever He was and whatever He was, He was for them. And after His ascension they thought of Him as for them toward God. You remember how Paul states it as the climax of what Jesus does for Christians. "It is Christ Jesus that died, yea rather, that was raised from the dead, who is at the right hand of God, who also maketh intercession for us."

Doubtless to some the idea of Jesus' intercession may be repugnant. Who wants an intercessor with his Father? Is it not a reflection on God's love? Did Jesus ever think of an intercessor with His God and Father? And has not Paul lapsed from Jesus' view of God to some lower view in which he was reared or which he learned in Gamaliel's classroom?

But when we pray for one another, do we cast a reflection on God's faithful thought and love? Are we reminding a forgetful Father or wheedling a reluctant Lord into more favorable consideration of human need? Are we not, rather, trying, like Moses, to be for them toward God—to look at God and them in the same view, to connect them with God and God with them? And could Paul or any other friend of Jesus imagine Him as doing anything else?

❧ THE LIVING LORD AND MASTER

A distinguished Jewish preacher in the city of Chicago, Dr. Solomon B. Freehof, has borne this striking witness to the power Christ affords His disciples:

The consciousness of the presence of God has come to millions of men and women through Jesus. . . . He is still the living comrade of countless lives. No Moslem ever sings, "Mohammed, lover of my soul," nor does any Jew say of Moses, the Teacher, "I need thee every hour". . . . Jesus brought God near to men through His presence. He makes the Divine personal for myriads of worshippers.

This is impressive testimony from a sympathetic outsider to that sense of adequacy through Christ for the quest of the impossible ideal voiced by an apostle: "I can do all things in Him that strengtheneth me."

Century after century the Jesus who was crucified has been for innumerable human souls the embodiment of the goal of life and of the path and power to its attainment. So inevitably the question rises: "Who is He?" Is He an accidental product of the cosmic process—one who chanced to come on the stage nearly two thousand years ago, and has chanced to maintain this unique hold over thousands in the generations since? Is He unconnected with the order of the cosmos itself?

Those who have yielded themselves to Him, and have known His disquieting, His guidance, His empowering, have never been content with such a casual explanation. They find themselves offering Him an homage beyond which they have naught to proffer. They accord Him their utmost reverence and fealty. God Most High can evoke no more from them. And for them Jesus is God manifest in Man—the Conscience not only of mankind, but also the Conscience in control of the universe. This is a leap of faith, but it is a leap which the vast majority of Christians have felt impelled to take. Such faith alone seems to do justice to One who reveals the goal of life, the way towards it, and furnishes power to attempt to reach it. In following Him they are persuaded that they have embarked on no uncertain quest and are enlisted in no losing cause. They are open-eyed to the obstacles which bar our progress, agreeing with Thomas Hardy that, "If way to the Better there be, it exacts a full look at the Worst."

They are never optimistic about contemporary triumph. From the day when an early disciple wrote: "The whole world lieth in wickedness," down to our own time when we are painfully aware of titanic forces assaulting the Christian ethic and a vast lethargy whelming its professed devotees, Christianity has seemed on the verge of collapse. Calvaries dot the course of human history; and there is no reason to fancy that the future on this planet will be easier than the past. But the cross has never been the end of a chapter in human affairs. It has marked the beginning of a further advance.

Here are men exposed to tragedy. Jesus Himself hangs at Golgotha, defeated and deserted. But that crucified Figure becomes to those who are mastered by Him the most revealing disclosure of ultimate Reality. Put side by side two sayings: "My God, why hast Thou forsaken Me?"—the feeling of the Sufferer Himself—and "God so loved the world"—the impression on those who have viewed the event in the light of its consequences. By the Crucified we are not only made ashamed of ourselves and our world; we are guided to live and labor in uttermost devotion, and empowered to hope and strive for a world penetrated and ruled by such love as He symbolises. If we cannot demonstrate to others that the universe is not uncaring, we can bear witness that it has not been so with us, that we have known a love given to us freely, beyond any human affection, and that our supreme inspirations come from the figure of Jesus.

✑ GOD'S TRANSFORMATION OF US

Earth does not renew itself in spring. It is lifted sunward in its orbit and the added degrees registered by the thermometer set in motion the whole process of repair. You and I come to the Lord's Table not mainly to do something, however admirable, but to have something done to and in us. We can learn much from the quietness of earth in the momentous days of spring. We have an idea that we must be up and busy, that as Christ's followers we have vast tasks to accomplish; and so we have. But the best things in our world are never made; they are grown. Poetry is grown in a human soul: its lines may be hammered out and polished; but no amount of diligent versifying will produce poetry; that springs from poetic soil. Friendships are never manufactured: they arise as from some latent seed, when congenial lives touch, and storm and sunshine help them to flourish and blossom and bear fruit. Christian lives are not achieved by effort of ours; they are grown by contact with the Sun of righteousness. The best service we render we shall never know of; the finest things we shall ever do will probably be unintended. It is our part to let God shine on us, warm us with His love, and renew us into His likeness. Let spring happen, and He will take care of the harvest. Here we remember Christ, think upon Him, and let God's light and love through Him fall on our minds and hearts that the miracle of spring may occur, and we be renewed.

And Paul lays special stress on the renewing of our *minds*. "The new man that is being renewed unto knowledge." "Be ye transformed by the renewing of your mind that ye may prove what is the good will of God." Spring is to come to our *heads* as well as our *hearts*. Lots of persons cherish the delusion that so long as they have good feelings it does not matter much what their opinions are. Paul knew that as a young man in Jerusalem he had had the finest of intentions and the most kindly of hearts but that he had been tragically mistaken, and had acted on the wrong side. We present ourselves at the Lord's Table to remember Jesus Christ in order that we may catch His point of view, see with His outlook, think with His mind. We are not renewed, unless our views—views of the people we have to do with, views of the work that is ours, views on the questions of the day, views of the experiences of life that we must encounter, experiences glad and sad, views of the living God, are thoroughly Christianized. How many Christian-hearted and un-Christian-headed people there seem to be! "Renewed unto knowledge," renewed in mind to discern the will of God—this is the springtide we need.

And Paul tells us that spring with Christians is not a season; it is a daily and continuous occurrence. "Therefore we faint not: but though our outward man is decaying, yet our inward man is renewed day by day." We lay stress on daily prayer, daily study of the Bible, daily thought of God, because the autumn and winter experiences of decay go on uninterruptedly, and these are ways to lift our spirits, as the earth is lifted in its orbit, closer to the Sun of our life. How cheering to recall that in our spirits there need be no autumn when life slackens, no winter when it sleeps! "Wherefore we faint not." The renewal that clothes the character with loveliness, that awakens the soul to pulsing vitality, that stimulates upspringing growth, is perpetual— "renewed day by day."

❧ APPROPRIATING THE GIFT OF GOD

Light may benefit us without our being aware of it, but bread must be eaten. No man becomes robustly Christian without constant effort, and the effort is not to make himself

Christlike—that would render him self-conscious. When we eat bread we do not think what it is going to do for us, and we do not have to think what we are going to do with it. We simply have to be hungry for it and take it. So a man must be hungry for Christ and so want Him that he appropriates Christ's spirit, His trust in God, His love that beareth, believeth, hopeth, endureth all and never faileth; and what will happen to him is no affair of his. Without our being aware of it, we shall lengthen in patience and broaden in sympathy, we shall grow in courage and hopefulness. We need not take our own measurements or weigh our characters. No doubt an occasional self-examination will not hurt us, but no man is capable of accurately calculating his stature or his weight. Others will find us larger in our natures, bigger-hearted, more sensitive in conscience, with a higher reach up and a longer reach out and a deeper reach down. And we shall not have stretched ourselves. Growth does not come by stretching; stretching strains. Growth comes by appropriating—taking in the light of the sun in food and drink, the Sun of righteousness in Christ. He nourishes us. His flesh is meat indeed and His blood is drink indeed.

There is still another connection between light and bread. Ask a chemist what food does in a human body, and he will answer: "It burns up, and supplies energy," and chemists measure the value of food in "calories" from the Latin word "calor" for heat. The flaming sun in the skies throws off its waves of whirling electrons to be caught and transformed into food, and this in turn becomes in us energizing fuel. Does not that form an apt illustration for Christ in the soul of man? The glowing heart of God sends down love, and this finds its embodiment and expression in Jesus, who by His self-offering on the cross becomes the food of man, and in those who receive Him He burns—the fuel of an ardent love like His own.

PRAYERS

O Father, whose unspeakable gift to us is Jesus Christ, the bread of heaven, we are not worthy so much as to gather up the crumbs which fall from Thy table, but Thou callest sinners unto repentance, and we hunger and thirst after righteousness. Centre our thoughts upon Christ, kindle our hearts by His love, constrain us by His cross to yield ourselves unto Him a living sacrifice, that we may have true communion with Thee, our Father, through Him, the way, the truth and the life.

O God, who satisfiest the longing soul and fillest the hungry soul with good and art Thyself the satisfaction of Thy children's needs, we thank Thee for the bread of heaven with which Thou daily feedest us, for the bread of home where the love of kindred incarnates Thine heart, for the bread of friendship where those who trust us and sympathise with us embody Thy companionship, for the bread of toil and the satisfaction useful labor gives all whose meat is to do Thy will and to accomplish Thy work, above all for Jesus Christ, the living bread from whom we find inspiration and strength to live with Thee as Thy children, and with all men as their devoted brethren, and to be with all Christians one body, one loaf on which the world is to feed and be filled with the Bread of God.

Bless to us this bread which we take in remembrance of Christ, and enable us so to share His life that Thou mayest dwell in us as Thou didst in Him.

Most holy and merciful Father, drawn by Thy gracious invitation and our own need we sinners come to this Thy table to think of Jesus Christ, our Lord and Saviour, and to feed in our hearts by faith on Him, the bread of heaven. We remember Him in the days of His flesh, made and tempted in all points like as we are, and praise Thee for His transforming friendship with sinful men and women, for the wisdom and grace of His words, the thoughtfulness and generosity in which He served, the courage and confidence in which He followed Thy will in life and death, and the love with which He bore, believed, hoped, endured all unfailingly. We remember that which we owe to Him: the knowledge of Thy fatherly goodness in His face, the redeeming touch of Thy hand through His cross, the shame He gives us for our sins, the strength He affords for our strains and labors, the assurance that in all things we are more than conquerors through His love.

Bless and sanctify with Thy Word and Spirit these thine own gifts of bread and wine, which we set before Thee, that we may by faith receive Christ crucified for us and evermore live in Him and He in us.

And here we offer and present unto Thee ourselves, to be a reasonable and living sacrifice, praying that through us and all who are one with us in the communion of Thy Church Christ may see of the travail of His soul and be satisfied.

And unto Him who loved us and loosed us from our sins in His blood and hath made us a kingdom to be priests unto his God and Father, be glory and dominion forever and ever.

Prayers through the Christian Year

❧ IN ADVENT

O God of hope, who hast awakened in all who have trusted Thee through the centuries a great expectation, who dost more than fulfil the hopes of the men of old in the coming of Jesus, and hast made Thy people look for even greater things, strengthen our confidence that every high and holy dream of men's hearts will be realized, and that the anticipation of Jesus Christ for the whole world will certainly come to pass. Enable us to look at every woe and wrong and error and unhappiness under the sun as doomed to disappear, and at every movement towards health and truth and justice and faith as sure to increase and succeed. And accounting no obstacle in men's prejudices or indifference or selfishness insuperable, may we resolutely set ourselves to prepare a highway for Thee into our world's life. May the Lord Christ find us and our fellow-countrymen a people made ready for Him with national ambitions and business standards and household ways of which He can approve, with churches and places of recreation and schools in which He can feel Himself at home.

O God, whose Son lived among us without sickness, though he bore in sympathy the sicknesses of others, we pray for all who are studying and striving to bring men into His complete physical health, for all scholars who give themselves to search out the causes and preventatives and cures of disease, for all physicians, surgeons and nurses who minister to the sick, for those who control and direct our hospitals, for those who build men's dwellings, furnish them with food, order the conditions of their work and rest, and for all who frame and administer our laws, that together we may labor for the bodily well-being of men and give Thee a race fit to achieve Thy purposes.

Most pitiful Father, unto whom are known the miseries of Thy children, we commend unto Thee those who have suffered through the ravages of war, those who are over-tasked in the world's work, the victims of vice and intemperance and greed, the unfortunates who have never had the inspirations of Christian homes and churches and friends to help them, the more unfortunate who possessing all these have sinned against light and against love, and all who by thoughtlessness or self-indulgence or laziness are failing to advance Thy cause and helping to keep the burden of wretchedness and pain and sin on their own and their brethren's lives. Come, O Lord Jesus, and let men see that in wounding the least of Thy brethren they are piercing Thee.

Lord God of the hopeful, we bless Thy name for those in every generation who have lived with their faces towards the sunrise, who have refused to be content with things as they were, who have possessed the love which believeth and hopeth all things and never faileth, whose eager eyes have welcomed each new ray of light here and been gladdened by the daybreak yonder and still look for the glorious light of the perfect day when Thy glory shall be revealed and all flesh shall see it together. Inspire us with their expectancy, and make us both to labor for and to depend confidently on Thee to grant us those things for which we pray with the trust of Jesus Christ.

~§ AT CHRISTMAS

Father of all, who didst gladden the home of Mary and Joseph by the coming of the Holy Child, make Him an abiding guest in our homes: binding our families together in mutual honor, confidence and service; banishing foolish pride of position, wasteful luxury, the self-indulgence which forgets the needs of those in want, and vain love of display; and consecrating our homes to Thy service so that each may be ruled by the single desire to advance Thy kingdom, that means, time, thought, health, our own and our dear ones' lives may be dedicated wholly to Thee for the fulfilment of Thy will for all men, in the name of Christ.

Blessed Lord, who hast caused the dayspring from on high to visit us, to give light to them that are in darkness and in the shadow of death and to guide our feet into the way of peace, we pray that the Spirit of good will may so fill the hearts of all of us who call ourselves Christians that our love may reflect the light of the world, drawing all men unto Him. Especially do we pray for the homeless, the friendless, the forgotten by all men, those who spend this day in prison, those whose rejoicing is unhallowed by any true consecration to Thee so that they know nothing of the great joy of possessing the Saviour, those for whom the day recalls memories of happier times now gone by, those who are lonely for loved voices hushed in death, those who have lost an earlier faith, and all who wish they could believe the message of this day, but find themselves unable. Grant that we who have learned the truth of the good tidings and have found in Jesus our Saviour deliverance from selfishness, distrust, and fear, may carry the gladness of this season throughout the year, rejoicing evermore because of Thine unspeakable gift in Him.

O God, who art faith and light and in whom is no darkness at all, as the world again recalls Thy tender mercy, whereby the dayspring from on high hath visited us, may all men come to His light and all nations be blessed with the brightness of His rising. May some fair star of hope guide the world's thinkers into His truth, its workers into His justice, its lawmakers into His righteousness, and all men into His love. Upon every place where Thy children dwell may the Sun of Righteousness arise with healing in His wings for all ills and woes, and may Christ be the light of earth as He is the light of heaven. May we and all children of the day, think, pray, toil and give that every man may be brought into the household of faith and the world become one holy family in which the Holy Child shall not be ashamed to call all of us His brethren.

◆§ AT THE END OF THE YEAR

Ancient of Days, whose years have no end, we, who are of yesterday and strangers and sojourners in the earth as all our fathers were, turn unto Thee, our dwelling-place in all generations. Amid the shadows that encompass us Thou art our everlasting light. In the midst of ceaseless changes Thou art the same and Thy compassions fail not. In every loss Thou remainest and we are continually with Thee. All things come to an end while from everlasting to everlasting Thou art God. Our flesh and our heart faileth, but Thou art the strength of our heart and our portion forever.

We have heard with our ears, O God, our fathers have told us, what work Thou didst in their days, in the days of old. Thy hand is not shortened that it cannot save, and before this year passes enable us to put off the old man with his doings—every selfish ambition, every bitterness, every failing to which we cling, conceit, prejudice, suspicion, fear—and to put on the new man in all Christlikeness of trust and sacrifice and hope, that henceforth it may be no longer we that live but Christ in us.

And we bless Thee that in a world where we must part from all we love, neither death nor life, nor things present nor things to come, nor height nor depth can separate us from Thy love in Christ Jesus our Lord; and we rejoice that we are even now in Thee in fellowship with those who have passed beyond the lapse of time and dwell in the city that hath foundations where there is no night. Teach us by the recollection of their faithful labor and valiant warfare to number our days, and looking not at things seen and temporal, but at things unseen and eternal to be careful for nothing save that we do Thy will, for the world passeth away and the lust thereof, but he that doeth the will of God abideth forever. And that will for ourselves and for all men we make our resolve and our prayer, as we say together after our Lord's commandment: Our Father—

Father, forgive, we beseech Thee, the stained record of the year that is gone. Enable us to forget things behind which hold us back in bitterness. Sift the ingatherings of our memories that evil may grow dim and good shine clearly. Keep us from narrow pride in outworn ways, blind eyes that will not see the good in change, impatient judgments of the experiments of others. Take from us all fear of the unknown future, since our times are in Thy hand, and Thou wilt not fail nor in any wise forsake us, through Jesus Christ our Lord.

O Father, who hast promised that as our days so shall our strength be, and who knowest the way that we take, if any of us are carrying loads which appear to weigh us down, remind us that Thy grace is sufficient for us; if any are careful and troubled about many things and anxious for the morrow, tell us that good works are afore-prepared that we should walk in them and that Thou wilt supply every need of ours according to Thy glorious riches in Christ; if any are lonely for comrades of other years, no longer with them, whisper to each: "The Lord, thy God, is with thee whithersoever thou goest." If any face failing health or increasing limitations, say unto them: "My strength is made perfect in weakness"; if any go into the untried future companionless, may they be found today of Him, the Friend that sticketh closer than a brother, Jesus Christ our Lord.

ᴇᴦ AT NEW YEAR'S

God of our life, in whose hand are our times, and whose providence has set us on the threshold of a new year, we renew our vows to Thee. We offer and present unto Thee our minds and consciences, our affections for kindred and for friends old and new, our loyalty to country and to the family of nations, our obligations to those who trust us, our opportunities for knowledge and service, our heritage in the Church of Christ, beseeching Thee to accept and employ us fully. Graciously pardon our unworthiness; discipline us to think and will according to the mind of Christ; fill us with Thy Holy Spirit in faith, in wisdom, in love. Reveal to us Thy truth as we think and learn, and by every experience fit us for the ministry of Thy people, through Him who is head over all things to the Church, Jesus Christ our Lord.

O Lord who from everlasting to everlasting art God and art the dwelling place of Thy children in all generations, receive us who through Jesus Christ, the Way, come to Thee our home and our Father. In the midst of a world where the years come and go, and we are but sojourners with no abiding city, grant us to dwell in Thee from whose love neither things present nor things to come, nor height nor depth, can separate us. Thy statutes are our songs in the house of our pilgrimage; and we pray Thee to stablish in us the loyalty which our vows proclaim, increase our faith, renew our obedience, prevent us from growing weary in well-doing, keep us in the secret place of Thy friendship, that through all our work in the world our life may be hid with Christ in God, our thoughts and consciences be lifted to heavenly levels, and our work be built into thine eternal purpose, through Jesus Christ our Lord.

❧ ON GOOD FRIDAY

O God, confront us with the cross of Christ, shaming us out of self-indulgence and love of luxury, sharpening our consciences to feel involved in every vice or wrong or pain, rendering intolerable to us unjust and needless inequalities, granting to every man a new sense of the sacredness of his work, of his brethren, of himself, inspiring commerce and industry and legislation with a heart akin to the Son of man's, lifting all education, science, and art to a loftier consecration, and transforming all men, the worst and the best, until all shall bear the marks of the Lord Jesus.

❧ AT EASTER

Lord of heaven and earth, in whose world goodness cannot die, nor truth be eclipsed in darkness, nor love holden of death, let the triumph of Jesus Christ put heart

235

and hope into all who are motivated by good will, all who trust in truth, all who share His conviction concerning Thee, all who use love as the supreme wisdom and most efficient force. Wherever throughout our world the Spirit of Jesus is pitted against ignorance or prejudice, unbelief or superstition, oppression or injustice, want of thought or want of heart, may we be quietly and patiently confident of His victory. Let our living hope ally us to Him both to work tirelessly and to wait expectantly for the establishment of His Kingdom when thou shalt be all in all.

Lord of life, from whom we come and unto whom we go, and from whose love neither death nor life nor things present nor things to come can separate us, help us to know that every follower of Christ is with Him alive unto Thee. To every soul whose thoughts go to some loved one's grave, let the angel of thy comfort say, "He is not here; he is risen." Lovely unto us were they in their lives; assure us that in Thy sight their deaths were precious, and may they mean no less to us now than in the days of their flesh. Convince us that Thou art still unfolding all the powers of the love it was ours to draw out here, and certify us that they still belong to us in Thee, O God unto whom all live.

O God, sought of all men and Seeker after all men, we rejoice that in Jesus man's search for Thee and Thy search for us meet. We adore Him, the Finder who dwelt in Thy love, and the Found in whom Thou didst dwell and through whom Thou art ever seeking us. Grant that we may be found of Thee and be Thine to possess, to use, to befriend, and also find Thee in Jesus, to be Thy sons and daughters forever.

❧ THE ASCENSION OF CHRIST

O God, the Father of Glory, who didst raise Jesus Christ from the dead and cause Him to share Thy throne, we rejoice in His exaltation. We praise Thee for our assurance in Him, that love attains the highest station, that self-sacrifice is crowned with glory and honor, that to do the will of God is to abide forever and share the triumph of Thy will. We thank Thee for our confidence that above the darkness and disasters of earth we can think of Jesus as supreme, and be of good courage that the saddest event shall ultimately work Thy purpose of love, as revealed in Him. And we beseech Thee, form in us His spirit of self-forgetfulness and self-consecration, that we may share His glory; and grant us ever to remember His enthronement that in doing His will we may know that with us is all power in heaven and earth.

O Father, in whose heaven Jesus has received the highest place and in whose earth He is more and more ascending to the dominion of all hearts, lift us in thought and life to share His spirit, that even now we may move in heavenly regions, even now wield the power of loving sympathy and service, even now be at home in Thee and have fellowship with all Thy faithful children in earth and heaven who abide in Thee forever.

❧ AT PENTECOST

O God, our Father, who in every age hast put Thy Spirit in prophet and apostle and warrior for righteousness, and hast been in that same Spirit the inspiration of the

237

faith and love of all the followers of Jesus, Thy Son, come in Him to the whole family of Thy children and grant us a world-wide Pentecost. Come as fire, burning up the impurities in men's thoughts and hearts, and kindling us to sacrificial service one of another; come as the rushing wind, filling lives with mighty power; come as the dove, quietly bringing trust in Thee and in men as Thy children. As in the beginning Thou didst move upon the face of the dark and waste waters and create a world of light and life, move through the ignorances and discords of our earth, and usher in that wished-for day when a new world shall stand before our eyes so bright and fair and rich in justice and kindness, in truth and faith, that Thou, its God, and all Thy like-minded children shall say it is good, and shout for joy. As in the Upper Room Thou camest upon the Church of Christ, bringing consecration and courage to win the world, and binding all hearts together in brotherly love, fill Thy Church universal today, giving every disciple a bold and skillful tongue to bear witness to Christ, drawing all Christians together in devotion to Thy purpose, and through them bringing in the common life of love.

God of our fathers, who hast enriched us with memories of patriots who laid down their lives to set our land at liberty and to keep it both free and united, grant Thy Holy Spirit to the President of the United States and all in authority, to us and all our fellow-citizens, that we may be public-spirited with the same devotion which has flamed in patriot hearts since our country's birth, and as a nation possess the Spirit of Christ, standing among all the peoples as one that serveth.

O God who by Thy one Spirit dost bind Christians in congregations, we remember the many members of this

Church who may be absent now, those who worship in other places, those who journey on the face of the great deep, those who are sick, beseeching Thee to grant them the joy of Thy presence and the light of Thy favor. We pray for lives lonely from recent sorrow, for minds distraught with financial perplexity, for those who watch their beloved suffer, for any who are unresponsive to the pleading of Thy Spirit's voice.

And we bless Thy name for that great company whom Thy good Spirit hath already led into a land of uprightness, rejoicing that our spirits still touch theirs in Thee, and praying that we may ever endeavor to maintain with them the unity of the Spirit by faithfully cleaving fast unto Thee with whom they dwell forever and ever.

ᛰᚦ FOR ALL SAINTS

O Lord, whose are all worlds, and in whose house are many mansions, we think with quiet thankfulness of faithful spirits who have passed from earth into the life eternal. Thine they were here, and Thine they remain yonder. We bless Thy name for our memories of them and for their bequest to us of high purposes and generous devotion. We thank Thee for our fellowship with them, and pray that our lives may be hid with Christ in Thee.

Grant, O God of saints, that compassed with so great a cloud of witnesses, we may be sharers of their trust in Thee, loyal to the heritage which they have bequeathed us, enabled to pass it on with increase to them who shall succeed us and to enter with them into that city where the Lamb is the everlasting light.

O King of saints, who hast not entered into Thy triumph alone but attended by ten thousand times ten thousand, we bless Thee for those with Thee whom we have known and loved. Let their presence on the heights draw us upwards as we toil and struggle, let their victory make us of good courage, let their faith and patience be our inspiration and our power, and by Thy grace may we too some day stand above all that today tempts and soils and casts us down, and in the heavenly places find our eternal home, through Jesus Christ our Lord.

◦⧉ INTERCESSIONS FOR THE TROUBLED AND THE SAD

O God our Father, who fillest the earth with Thy loving kindness, we commend unto Thee the tired, the suffering, the sad, the burdened and the sinning, those who have met with some keen disappointment or who bear the pain of being unjustly dealt with, those whom man's hardness drives into distrust of Thy love, those who have been embittered by failures, or made self-confident by successes, and all who live without Christ, the guide and strength and inspiration of men.

And we give Thee thanks for lives at rest, for every heart that loved righteousness and every mind that looked to things of others and every soul that walked humbly with Thee, for whom heaven has opened to receive new riches in their characters, who now dwell with the saints in light. Grant that we may be followers of their work of faith and labor of love and patience of hope and enter with them into Thy purposes for the earth here, and thus be at home with them and Thee forever.

O Father of Mercies, we bring Thee those who are in our thoughts, the lonely, the tired, the sick, those who have lost the light of reason, the embittered through disappointment and the hardened through success, those who have not learned to forget themselves in the service of others, the defeated by opposing circumstances, the disheartened by frequent failure, the scarred by conflict, and all those most to be pitied who are no longer in the battle but have surrendered to forces they felt too strong to combat. Use us, O Lord, to aid Thee in bringing our brethren to victorious sonship through Christ our Lord.

Thur. eve

O Thou who art unto all Thy children a hiding-place from the wind and a covert from the tempest, as streams of water in a dry place and the shade of a great rock in a weary land, as we place in Thy shelter any known to us in sickness, temptation, sorrow, perplexity, loneliness or any trouble, enable us as Thy sons and daughters to be to our brethren a protection and refreshment, that from us they may draw Thy calm and courage and comfort and compassion. And if to Thine all-seeing eyes there be any here who know not the desires of their own hearts, interpret them to themselves that they go hence seeking to be made more near to the likeness of our Elder Brother, Jesus Christ.

Fri. eve

Gracious Father, we place in Thy safekeeping those dear to us, present and absent, those known and unknown to us whose labor ministers to our wellbeing, whose studies add to our knowledge, or whose examples quicken us to more generous thought and act, or whose prayer and devotion sanctify us to a godlier life. We commit to Thy wise and tender hands any of whom we are thinking in sickness or sorrow, minds that have lost the light of reason, souls without the lamp of faith, the pitiful company who vainly look for work by which to earn their bread and the more tragic company of those who have never been claimed for partnership in their Father's business, nor tasted his goodness and grace.

And we bless Thy name for the faithful of all the ages, who shone as lights in their generation and now dwell in that city to which Christ is the unsetting sun. And we beseech Thee to keep us one in faith with Thy Church on earth, one in hope with Thy Saints in heaven, and one in love with Thy children everywhere, through Jesus Christ, the Saviour and Lord of all.

✌ THANKSGIVINGS

O Thou who inhabitest the praises of Israel, we enter Thy gates with thanksgiving. For this fair world with its ever-surprising beauty in earth and sky and ocean, for homes where love believes in us so implicitly that we are ashamed to be false to its trust and disappoint its expectations, for friends who gladden us with their companionship, enrich us with their sympathy and inspire us to make the best of ourselves, for useful daily work, for those who need us and give meaning to our daily life, for Thy constant training through our blunders and failures, through disappointments and success, above all for Jesus Christ in whom we see Thee our God and ourselves as Thou meanest us to become, we bless Thy name. Let Thy goodness lead us to repentance and Thy love shame us from our selfishness. Let the recalling of Thy benefits make us dedicate ourselves to Thy service, through Jesus Christ our Lord.

God of light, by whom the sun ariseth and man goeth forth unto his work and to his labor until the evening, we give Thee thanks for the renewal of sleep, for the trust of another day despite our misuse of our yesterdays, for challenging tasks and enriching studies, for comrades of our spirits who double our joys by sharing them, for our fellowship through books with thinkers past and present, for hearts who cherish us and lift our names in prayer, for our heritage through thy Church with millions of Christ's followers throughout the earth and with ten thousand times ten thousand who have entered the larger life of the city of God. By all these Thy common mercies and singular favors consecrate us to live this day as loyal disciples of our Lord and Saviour Jesus Christ.

Sat. eve

O God, Thou comest to meet us along many paths, in the beauty and bounty of each new day, in the comradeship of friends, in every glimpse of truth, in every call of duty, in every stirring of sympathy within our hearts, in every penitence for sin. And Thou comest to us yet more clearly and movingly in Thy sanctuary and speakest to us through the heritage of Thy Church where believers of many generations have enshrined their experiences in hallowed scriptures and in hymns, and where with kindred spirits we adore Thee manifest for us in the face of Jesus Christ. Before Thee our souls acknowledge Thy numberless kindnesses: thanks be unto Thee, O God. Before Thee we offer ourselves afresh to be used in Thy service: show us Thy way for us and render us obedient unto the heavenly vision, through the grace of Christ, in whose name we pray.

An index of first lines of Prayers immediately follows.

✑ INDEX OF FIRST LINES OF PRAYERS

Prayers for the Seasons of the Church Year will be found on pages 229-240.